Business
Ethics

Business Ethics

A Case Study
Approach

STEPHEN K. HENN

WILEY

John Wiley & Sons, Inc.

Copyright © 2009 by Stephen K. Henn. All rights reserved.

Published by John Wiley & Sons, Inc., Hoboken, New Jersey.

Published simultaneously in Canada.

No part of this publication may be reproduced, stored in a retrieval system, or transmitted in any form or by any means, electronic, mechanical, photocopying, recording, scanning, or otherwise, except as permitted under Section 107 or 108 of the 1976 United States Copyright Act, without either the prior written permission of the Publisher, or authorization through payment of the appropriate per-copy fee to the Copyright Clearance Center, Inc., 222 Rosewood Drive, Danvers, MA 01923, 978-750-8400, fax 978-646-8600, or on the web at www.copyright.com. Requests to the Publisher for permission should be addressed to the Permissions Department, John Wiley & Sons, Inc., 111 River Street, Hoboken, NJ 07030, 201-748-6011, fax 201-748-6008, or online at http://www.wiley.com/go/permissions.

Limit of Liability/Disclaimer of Warranty: While the publisher and author have used their best efforts in preparing this book, they make no representations or warranties with respect to the accuracy or completeness of the contents of this book and specifically disclaim any implied warranties of merchantability or fitness for a particular purpose. No warranty may be created or extended by sales representatives or written sales materials. The advice and strategies contained herein may not be suitable for your situation. You should consult with a professional where appropriate. Neither the publisher nor author shall be liable for any loss of profit or any other commercial damages, including but not limited to special, incidental, consequential, or other damages.

For general information on our other products and services, or technical support, please contact our Customer Care Department within the United States at 800-762-2974, outside the United States at 317-572-3993 or fax 317-572-4002.

Wiley also publishes its books in a variety of electronic formats. Some content that appears in print may not be available in electronic books.

For more information about Wiley products, visit our Web site at http://www.wiley.com.

Library of Congress Cataloging-in-Publication Data:

Henn, Stephen K., 1963–
   Business ethics : a case study approach / Stephen K. Henn.
      p. cm.
   Includes bibliographical references and index.
   ISBN 978-0-470-45067-3 (cloth)
  1.   Business ethics–Case studies. I. Title.
   HF5387.H4645 2009
   174'.4—dc22

                             2009005649

Printed in the United States of America.

10 9 8 7 6 5 4 3 2 1

Contents

Preface

What lies behind us and what lies before us are tiny matters compared to what lies within us.

—Ralph Waldo Emerson

JANUARY 1, 2009

When I set out to write a book about ethics in the summer months of 2008, I did not imagine what lay ahead for the world economy by year's end. The financial crisis, the seemingly intractable problems facing Detroit, the Bernie Madoff Ponzi scheme, the Siemens bribery scandal that resulted in an $800 million fine, and other developments have altered the business and economic landscape for the foreseeable future. Ethics seems to be discussed frequently when people talk about these matters. One hears "moral hazard" a lot. The substantive discussion, however, should be "Have we learned our lesson?" If the past few years are any guide, the answer is no.

In the seven years since Enron exploded, it seems little has changed. In the oft-cited *2007 National Business Ethics Survey,* the Ethics Resource Center observed corporate misbehavior is up since 2001. Despite all the words and regulations aimed at building ethical and responsible organizations, misbehavior has increased. As someone who has observed organizations' attempt to address corporate misconduct, this comes as no surprise. This is not to say corporate America is inherently bad. It is not. And there has been progress. But three factors conspire to stifle it. First, during the post-Enron period, it took time to figure out what government regulators and the Department of Justice wanted. Unfortunately, whenever the government steps into the fray and declares its intent to use the power of the state to effect change, those potentially affected wait to see what the rules are going to be. Given what happened to Arthur Andersen because of its role in Enron, KPMG because of its sale of tax shelters, the effect of the McNulty memorandum on attorney-client privilege, and the like, just *what* appropriate action to take was unclear. Time and experience have provided some guidance. The Federal Sentencing Guidelines and the Committee of Sponsoring Organizations of the Treadway Commission—COSO—have provided an integrated framework, but not absolute assurance.

The second factor is what is meant by ethics. This question has two dimensions. The first relates to the natural feeling that all of us are ethical up to—and past—the point where we commit fraud. When the facts are all out, Bernie Madoff probably did not get up one morning and say, "Life is a bit too goody-goody for me. I think I'll run a Ponzi scheme and defraud investors of $50 billion, give or take." In the vast majority of cases, there is something small that starts to snowball. A corporation needs to cover a greater-than-expected loss, so it moves some money around and books some sketchy entries. The enabling lie is something to the effect of "We will be okay, because we will correct it next quarter." But things do not go well the next quarter and doubling down the next quarter only exacerbates the problem. The malfeasor is now stuck and either has to own up to the mistake or let it ride again . . . and again until the problem becomes too big and collapses under its own weight. Guilt can be like a ton of bricks and then some.

The second dimension is measurement. How do we measure the lack of ethics and how that may affect us one day? After all, are we not interested in the risk that something unethical can take place as well as whether our record is clean to date? Even if the defenses against fraud have protected the organization thus far, are they adequate to protect us in the future? Developing quantitative measures for qualitative data is never easy, but several methodologies have been developed to benchmark where an organization is and measure changes. As these tools become prevalent and accepted, standards can be developed for companies and organizations.

The final factor is the one that concerns us now. Too many organizations address the symptoms, not the disease. The chances for unethical behavior can be minimized with an understanding of why good people make bad ethical choices. An organization does not make mistakes; people within that organization do. Organizations do not commit fraud; people within that organization make the decision—alone or in concert—to commit fraud. In my experience, in today's politically correct world, not enough attention is paid to the individual choices people make within an organization. Yet in each case of corporate malfeasance, a point exists at which one or more individuals choose between doing the right thing or doing the wrong thing. In this book, we look at why individuals make the choices they do; what role the organization plays in their decision making, and what is the often misunderstood role of leadership in affecting behavior. I hope that by the last chapter you understand the background necessary to start developing specific action plans for your organization.

THE BIGGEST LOSER

As an ethics professional, I have much in common with a personal fitness trainer. This analogy works on many levels. While some clients are fit and trim from an ethical perspective, most organizations run the gamut from mildly to morbidly obese. To a personal trainer, weight loss is quite simple: Do you expend more calories than you consume? The physical formula is also simple: Reduce the calories you consume through diet and increase the calories you expend through exercise.

Of course, it is not that easy. Despite the inherent benefits of being fit, such as health and self-esteem, experience tells us that it is very difficult to battle the bulge. The biggest challenge to overcome is not opportunity, but mind-set. The secret to reducing weight lies in changing mental perceptions and attitude. Often it is phrased in terms of altering your lifestyle. Get away from the things, situations, and people that cause you to overeat and neglect exercise. Break the bad habits and keep them broken. Quite frankly, most people would rather take a pill and be done with it. Dieting is no fun and exercise is hard, so do them tomorrow. Or you fool yourself into thinking one donut won't make a difference. Or you think, I have been good and I deserve a reward: Then you go to Starbucks—"One large Frappuccino, please." But your body cares only about the world as it is and not the world you wish for, so that Frappuccino will take about five miles of walking at a brisk pace, just to get back to even.

Creating an ethical organization faces similar hurdles. Too many organizations are looking for a quick solution, a "pill." Too many consultants are perfectly willing to sell an organization a bottle of Hoodia or other limited solution. ("Watch the pounds melt away in just five minutes a day! Guaranteed!") The result is that organizations are no better off than they were before Enron made "business ethics" an oxymoron.

WHY YOU?

This is a book designed for senior leaders of organizations: boards, C-level executives, trustees, managing partners, government officials— anyone tasked with a duty, fiduciary or otherwise—to govern an organization. Of course, others should read it. The lessons learned here would not be lost on anyone, whether they are inside an organization or as an outside stakeholder. Nevertheless, I wrote this book to start a dialogue among senior leadership levels about the tactical issues relating to ethics and ethical behavior in organizations.

Further, this book is written with the assumption that you are concerned about the impact of ethical or unethical behavior on your organization. Some leaders do not see ethics as an important part of an organization's fabric, or they only care for image reasons. Commitment counts. Like it or not, your organization has a hypersensitive B.S. detector and any attempt to pretend ethics is important to the organization, but not to you, is doomed and may even backfire.

Employees in your organization follow leadership and can only be as serious about ethics as you are. Ethics for *thee*, but not for *me* is a recipe for failure.

This book is not simply about business or corporate ethics. There is no such distinction. There is "ethics" plain and simple. While we often talk about business ethics and business ethics is very much in the spotlight—ethical behavior is also an issue for professional firms such as accountants and lawyers, nonprofits, universities, and government, indeed anywhere large groups of individuals work toward a common goal. Therefore, we will discuss examples of malfeasance in a number of different contexts and business is only one of them.

This is not a survey book. While we look at history and several contextual case studies—positive and negative—germane to ethical behavior, we also discuss in depth how to approach and resolve specific ethical situations using the ideas in this book. We learn how to recognize warning signs and how to distinguish yellow flags from red.

Real organizations are dynamic and deep. Given the uniqueness of each organization, there is no simple checklist to determine the level of exposure your organization has to unethical behavior. This is not a how-to book. It is a set of tools to use your own judgment and understanding. Let's face it: You are where you are because something inside you has guided you along a successful path. This book focuses your attention on the key issues that underlie ethical and unethical behavior and provide you with the basic underpinnings to apply your judgment to each situation as it arises.

WHAT LIES AHEAD

This book gives both a theoretical and practical perspective on organizational ethics. Chapter 2 is a discussion on why business ethics is important. While "being good for goodness sake" is admirable, there is also growing empirical evidence that suggests organizations built on strong ethical foundations outperform organizations where ethics is not a principal business driver. Chapter 3 discusses why ethics is such an issue for all kinds of organizations—and not just businesses and corporations—that are the subject of scrutiny. Chapter 4 gives a historical view of the evolution of ethics and how that has shaped our understanding of its importance in business.

The next three chapters discuss key elements involved in ethical and unethical behavior. Not every possible driver of human behavior is covered, but the focus here is on those most likely to impact your organization. Going to the notion of controllable versus uncontrollable risk, we look at the elements that are both controllable and common. Chapter 5 discusses the psychology behind individual decision making with an eye toward understanding both general moral development and specific stresses. Chapter 6 talks about the role that group behavior plays in affecting individual decision making and how to strengthen an individual's affinity for your organization. Chapter 7 is about leadership and the critical role leaders play in determining the culture of the organization.

Chapter 8 discusses the role of trust in an organization and its internal and external dealings. Chapters 9 through 11 discuss steps that can be taken to structurally reduce risk. First, how to minimize exposure, then how to create an environment that reinforces ethics, and finally the role of leadership—broadly defined—and how that impacts behavior.

Case studies in each chapter give basic facts germane to the discussion, followed by discussion. Some cases will be familiar and some will be new, but it is hoped that each will be meaningful. Finally, we discuss what would have been the right course of action, but depending on the objective, focusing on what were the warning signs and what was missing to allow for a better outcome.

Acknowledgments

Talent wins games, but teamwork and intelligence win championships.

—MICHAEL JORDAN

While there is one name on the cover of this book, a number of people contributed to this book and made for a much better story. First, I would like to thank Anjali Gupta for her help and guidance. At critical points, when a push or research was needed, Anjali stepped up and provided help. I was lucky enough to have a tremendous team to help on researching case studies. In addition to Anjali, I would like to thank Katherine Liposky, Roberto Scalese, Prema Srivanasan, and Wendy Williams for their efforts in researching a number of the case studies. Anjali, Kat, Berto, Prema, and Wendy, with the contributions of Marni Centor and the invaluable assistance of Joyce Liposky, formed the "book club" that set the tone and approach as this project got off the ground.

Next, I would like to thank the staff at John Wiley & Sons, in particular Stacey Rivera, for their patience with me and the guidance I received.

Finally, this book would not have come about without the support of my wife Alison and my family. She serves as the moral leader of our family and I cannot find a better living example of integrity.

CHAPTER 1

Introduction

To see what is in front of one's nose needs a constant struggle.

—GEORGE ORWELL

THEMES

So, with some niceties dispensed with, let's spend time on the over-arching themes that you should keep in mind as we go through this discussion. The first is that your organization is not perfect, nor will it ever be. There will always be some risk involved. With employee turnover in the range of 10 to 20 percent per year, you will always be adding new dynamics to the mix of your personnel structure. This obvious fact goes to the point that you need to be looking at the ethical makeup of your organization constantly in the same manner and rigor you review financial performance.

So it is important to understand what you can control and what you cannot control. To keep it simple, there are three basic types of unethical behaviors. The first is the "lone wolf," that is, someone acting alone in a position of trust and in an area of their expertise. Embezzlement is typical of this problem. It is hard to stop the determined lone wolf. The good news is that the damage is *usually* minimal. The slightly better news is that this unethical behavior is not "structural." It is the ethics equivalent of getting struck by lightning. Bad luck, but you move on. We will talk about ways—in the context of preventing more substantial problems—to minimize risk. A determined person, however, will be difficult to spot. That is, until they drive the $80,000 sports car to work.

The next type of unethical behavior is the "oops," which is far more common. This is where an employee—loyal, hardworking, and honest—makes a mistake. A big one. A mistake that could get him or her fired. The decision then, on that person's part, is to fess-up or cover-up. The overwhelming temptation is to cover-up and hope for the best. The "oops," like the lone wolf, is usually not fatal or structural. Yet how the scenario plays out will heavily influence future behavior.

The last type is the "conspiracy." As the term implies, it is the effort by more than one individual to perpetuate a fraud. These latter two situations are the primary focus of this book. These situations are the *company killers*. Conversely, they should be the easiest to prevent to a diligent organization: The bigger the conspiracy, the greater the risk to the conspirators that they involve someone who exposes the conspiracy.

Second, while a qualitative concept, ethics can be measured. Ethical and unethical behavior show up in costs, growth, employee turnover, employee satisfaction, and, of course, return on equity. Attitudes can be surveyed and the results compared over time and across your organization. While there is a temptation to dismiss qualitative results as too soft, there are a number of methodologies and tools that can analyze behavior and produce actionable data.

Finally, since this is not fiction, I don't mind revealing a key plot point early. As you read this, keep in mind the notion of "trust." Trust is so important to an organization at the macro- and microlevel that it is essential to discuss upfront. The reason we focus on personal ethical behavior and the aggregate ethical behavior of an organization is because it is the basis of building trust between individuals and between organizations. At the core, trust is the most essential way to reduce cost and build value.

As mentioned in the preface, throughout the book there are case studies and examinations of ethical lapses that focus on the role of the senior executives. I urge you to examine these situations with an eye toward identifying the breakdown of trust in the relationships. This is important because, while trust is a "touchy feely" concept, as senior executives you often do not have enough raw data to understand the facts well enough. In point of fact, where issues of fraud and malfeasance are involved, real facts are even *harder* to come by as they are often covered up or obfuscated by those perpetuating the unethical behavior.

What you are left with is a gut feeling for the situation: Do you trust the facts? Do you trust the statements? Do you trust the individuals? If not, it is time to act.

CASE STUDY — **A CFO'S DILEMMA**

Years ago, there was a chief financial officer (CFO) of a manufacturing company about to be taken public. Times were good: The company had successfully come out of the development stage and started to ship product, had negotiated relationships with the top resellers in our industry and, in so doing, secured upward of 85 percent of the distribution chain, and the initial reception from the investment banking community was very good. The company was buzzing with excitement—especially as employees and management started to believe their stock options would be worth a fair amount of money.

The accounting group and outside auditors had recently completed the audit of the second-quarter numbers that would be used as the basis for the offering. Summer was upon them and there was a lull in the activity as the company was in the final stages of deciding on an investment banker. Returning from lunch one day, the CFO saw a tractor-trailer at the loading dock. This was good news because it meant the company was shipping product. Taking a quick detour, the CFO asked the manufacturing manager

(Continued)

where the product, a specialized machine, was headed. "Here," he said. "It is coming back for a software upgrade. It will be going back out in the next day or so." Oh, well, the CFO thought, and headed to his office.

But something nagged at him. The company's processes included a fairly detailed forecast of revenue, and the CFO did not recall anyone forecasting upgrade revenue for the foreseeable future. Later in the day, curiosity getting the better of him, the CFO went back down to the manufacturing manager and asked if he knew if the software upgrade had been forecasted and for when—the CFO's assumption being that this machine was being upgraded early. "No, we are not charging for this. It's included in the sales price. But it is no big deal; it costs us nothing. Plug in a computer and press a button; maybe 20 minutes of work," he said.

The CFO had negotiated the contracts when he was an outside advisor to the company, and he was damn certain that there were no "free" software upgrades. The CFO stated, "I am fairly certain upgrades were not included in the price."

"Beats me, but I know this machine is getting an upgrade."

This could be a very big problem. The company recognized the revenue based on acceptance of the device. If there was an expectation of an upgrade, there could not be acceptance. No acceptance, no revenue. Having just completed the audit, the CFO knew the company had booked the revenue for all machines shipped to date.

The CFO pored over his files, but there was nothing in the files to indicate the upgrade was due. The CFO then tried to contact the head of engineering, but he was away on vacation. The nagging feeling would not go away, so the CFO went down to the head of engineering's office and grabbed the chief engineer's customer file. In it was a letter—a one-paragraph letter—agreeing to the upgrades. The CFO made a copy and went back to his office. Sitting there, the CFO must have read the letter dozens of times looking for a way out. More correctly, he was looking for an easy way out. There was no way around it: The letter meant that the company needed to restate its revenue. Thankfully, the company had not disclosed anything publicly, but that was a silver lining to a very dark cloud. The CFO thought about the financial impact on the company and the delay in the IPO; he thought about the impact on the employees and their stock options; and the CFO thought about his stock options.

The CFO also thought about how he was the only one who knew there was a problem.

On the one hand, it was pretty clear to him there was no intentional mischief. The engineers who started the company did not appreciate the implications of the letter (there was no CFO, controller, or accountant when the letter was signed) and the company had grown from a dozen engineers to a staff of over 100 in two years, so a software upgrade must have seemed trivial in the grand scheme of things. The accounting rule was pretty straightforward; but until the CFO's coincidental run-in on the dock, neither side thought to communicate with the other. There were a thousand reasons why this was an innocent mistake.

But none of that alleviated the impact.

LEADERSHIP POINT OF VIEW

The CFO is faced with a difficult blend of circumstances, yet one that is highly illustrative for our purposes. It is easy to say what should have been done, but the right decision is not an easy one to make. First, there are three things going through the CFO's mind as he sat in his office—three things that were making him choose to shut his mouth. The first was money: The decision to come clean would cost a lot to the company, his fellow employees, and to him. While the first two were very important, let's be honest, the thought of the pot of IPO gold being pushed away weighed heavily on his mind. The IPO payoff was important to him for a variety of reasons: Long hours would be rewarded, a second child was on the way, and that new-car smell is very enticing.

The second thought going through his mind was that he could get away with not speaking up. As a successful

(Continued)

executive, the CFO would never be accused of having a small ego and the voice in his head was in full chest-puffing mode: He could deflect questions, nuance answers if necessary, and, if worse came to worse, tear up the copy and enjoy plausible deniability. Ego is a critical factor because it told him he would not get caught.

Finally, he was afraid of the consequences of speaking up. What would this do to his standing in the company? Would he get fired? The CFO kept thinking, "This is not my fault," but his conscience would answer, "But it is your responsibility." He did not have to be an ethics expert to realize that he was *not* going to be viewed as a conquering hero. Everyone in the company looked forward to cashing in, and it would be pretty clear that Mr. Goody Two Shoes spoiled the party. In addition, *nobody* would understand why. It was some arcane accounting rule that would not make sense because the cost of the impact far exceeded the cost of the upgrade.

The Conclusion

The CFO reported the situation to the president and was met with that look all CFOs have seen at one time or another . . . the "you have got to be kidding me" look. No one was pleased with the news, least of all the external auditors. Fortunately, there was no consideration given to any alternative and the company restated the financials. The IPO was delayed, pushing it back four months into a much less receptive market, which had a large impact on the financial health of the company and the value of the employee holdings.

In the end, the CFO made the right decision for the simplest of reasons. First, he was confident that he was doing the right thing, and that his boss would support the decision. The company's culture was a "no nonsense," "reality wins" environment. The CFO had seen the approach taken with the numerous engineering challenges the company had to overcome. He knew, too, while there would be a lot of unhappiness with the news, getting that news out and deal with it was the approach the company took when dealing with problems. He was sure this accounting challenge would be no different.

Part of that confidence stemmed from the fact that the company and management were fair to a fault. The company did not apply one set of rules to govern the behavior of lower-level employees and another for senior employees. In fact, it was often the top management who sacrificed for the good of the company as a whole. Further, it was a company built upon past personal and professional friendships and associations, so it was imperative right from the start to make it clear that we are all expected to act and be treated in the same way to prevent factions or cliques from developing.

Finally, the CFO came to the personal conclusion that it is easy to be a leader in good times, but his professional ambition was to be a leader through it all. He had built the accounting team upon the principles of professionalism, and now was the time to step up and show what that meant. He knew standing up for the right thing would build trust in the eyes of his staff, management, auditors, and the investment banker. Doing the wrong thing would destroy that trust. That trust, be it personal, professional, or corporate, could be needed in the future.

The course of action was taken based on three interwoven factors. First, while the situation was very stressful, the CFO was personally comfortable that the organization would be fair and supportive. *Doing the right thing was not a threat to his job.* Second, the behavior of the organization and groups within the organization consistently sought to get things right in every area. The "reality wins" message was hammered home in each department and at every level. Finally, the CEO led the organization with great personal integrity and expected others to act in the same manner. To act otherwise would have been a disappointment. The right decision was made because of individual security, group pressure to always do the right thing, and leadership integrity. Creating this environment is your goal.

CHAPTER 2

Why Are Ethics Critical?

Ut sementem feceris, ita metes. (As you sow, so shall you reap.)

—CICERO

WHAT IS THE OBJECTIVE?

Executive leadership is certainly under constant pressure to produce results. At the end of 2008 and heading into 2009, there is little reason to expect the pressure to let up anytime soon. As much as American businesses have been accused of managing for the next quarter's numbers, the current economic conditions place a premium on demonstrably well-managed businesses. "Demonstrably," in this case, means making it crystal clear to the market that the business is prepared to weather the economic downturn.

Of course, this criterion seems to apply in good times as well as bad. The issue is not profitability or revenue, but performance relative to other alternatives. Is your company performing better than the competition? Is it performing better than other industries? Is it performing better than other investment alternatives? Nonprofits and nongovernmental organizations (NGOs) are not immune. The metrics may be different, but any organization dependent on cash received from outside sources—be it a customer, shareholder, or donor—is being evaluated on the "return" on those dollars coming in.

So let us get the premise out on the table: Business ethics is about high-performance companies. Business ethics is not about simply "doing good," as if some public altruism is going to make the market more tolerant of bad management, poor financial performance, or substandard return on investment. Business ethics is about the structural health of an organization and the ability of an organization to outperform its competition. Organizations that integrate ethics into the fiber of the organization will gain a competitive advantage. These organizations will be able to reduce the cost of doing business, not just in terms of reduced risk of lawsuits, fines, or other costs of malfeasance, but by reducing natural impediments that arise from a dysfunctional environment. Further, ethical organizations attract commerce and, arguably, attract it at a premium. This is common sense: Would you rather deal with a crook or someone trustworthy? Given the choice, how much more would you pay to avoid the risk? So, while you may have the best intentions of creating an ethical atmosphere at your organization—and you should be commended—first and foremost, business ethics is about *enhancing organizational performance.*

The Research

For many years, there was little, if any, research done on comparing ethical businesses with peer companies. First off, how do you define "ethical"? Is there a consistent standard as to what constitutes "social responsibility"? What does it mean for a company to be "sustainable"? Does each mean the same thing if you are a utility as opposed to an electronics manufacturer or Web services firm? Does an organization need to pursue "all of the above" to have an impact or is pursuing just one goal enough? Given the price tag, why is compliance with Sarbanes-Oxley and the Federal Sentencing Guidelines not good enough?

The concepts have evolved over the past few years to the point where answers are more concrete than before. While there is still some jockeying in the ethics industry, the ideals are being standardized and, with the level of awareness raised, a variety of research was conducted that supports the contention that ethical business practices provide significant long-term benefits to the organization.[1] Among the benefits of adopting ethical and responsible business practices, as cited by the advocacy group Business for Social Responsibility, are:

- *Improved financial performance.* Companies listed on the Dow Jones Sustainability Index and those on the 2001 Business Ethics Best Citizen list performed significantly better than their peers.

- *Enhanced brand image and reputation.* Businesses are finding that customers, banks, and insurers are more favorably disposed to companies with an image of responsible behavior. This enhanced image produces more sales, increases access to capital, and lowers risk. Surveys indicate that social responsibility ranks above brand reputation and business fundamentals when customers are seeking a product or service.

- *Increased sales and customer loyalty.* Companies perceived as socially and environmentally responsible are more likely to experience increased sales and profitability compared to their peers. Surveys indicate that as many as 80 percent of Americans take corporate citizenship into account when making purchases.

- *Increased productivity and quality.* Better working conditions and lower environmental impacts translate to increased productivity and a lower error rate in the workplace. The result is far fewer defective products and greatly reduced costs in handling customer complaints.

- *Increased ability to attract and retain employees.* Prospective employees are likely to evaluate a company's behavior toward the environment and the company's values prior to signing on for a career. A survey by the Aspen Institute Initiative for Social

Innovation through Business confirmed this. It found that over 50 percent of MBA students would seek another job if there was a conflict between their values and those of the business where they worked.

- *Reduced regulatory oversight.* Government agencies are likely to reward organizations that have a record of proactive efforts that carry beyond mere compliance. The result is that companies that are considered more responsible are subject to fewer inspections and less paperwork.

- *Access to capital.* Investments in socially responsible companies are growing at a rate well beyond that being experienced by their peers. For example, investing in companies screened for social concerns grew from $1.49 trillion in 1999 to $2.03 trillion in 2001, accounting for about 12 percent of all investments under professional management in the United States.

Additionally, research conducted by the Institute of Business Ethics has shown that companies with a clear commitment to ethical conduct outperform those that do not. This study, conducted in the United Kingdom, explored indicative measures of ethical commitment and corporate responsibility and then compared them against financial performance measures over a period of four years. In this way, the research investigated whether it can be shown that a commitment to business ethics does pay. Seven indicators were chosen—four of corporate financial performance—market value added (MVA), economic value added (EVA), price earnings ratio (P/E ratio), and return on capital employed (ROCE)—and three of corporate responsibility—having a code of ethics, ratings for managing social and ethical risks, and being cited consistently in the annual list of Britain's Most Admired Companies. The sample consisted of between 41 and 86 U.K. companies divided into two cohorts: those that have had codes of ethics[2] for five years or more and those that explicitly said they did not. A review of similar research shows that the relationship between good financial performance and other indicators of corporate responsibility, such as environmental management, corporate social responsibility and sustainability, is positive but not definitive.

This new study sought to find out whether or not the presence of an ethical code could be used as an indicator of genuine ethical commitment. Good practice for a sample of U.K. companies, with and without a code, was tested by looking at a rating for risk management and a peer evaluation, which included, for example, competent management, financial soundness, and quality of goods and services. The research drew several conclusions. First, the presence of an ethical code is an indicator of genuine ethical commitment, though, as seen with Enron, not an absolute guarantee of ethical action. Second, a positive correlation exists between an accessible ethical code and financial performance.

The study went further and looked at whether having an accessible ethical code had an impact on the relationship between ethical commitment and financial performance over the four-year period. When measured on financial performance, three of the four measures of corporate financial performance values used in this study—EVA, MVA, and P/E ratio—were found to be higher for those companies with a code of ethics compared to a similar-sized peer group that did not have any code of ethics for the period from 1997 until 2001. Further, companies with a code of ethics generated significantly more economic-added value and market-added value in the period from years 1997 until 2000 than those without codes of ethics. In addition, companies with a code of ethics experienced far less P/E ratio volatility over a four-year period than those without codes of ethics. This data suggest that they may be a more secure investment in the longer term. Finally, with regards to ROCE, companies with codes of ethics were clearly superior performers over the four-year period. While little discernable difference was found in return on capital for those companies with or without a code for the first two years, from 1999 to 2001 there was an approximately 50 percent increase in the average return on capital employed by those companies with explicit codes of ethics, while the return on capital employed for those companies without a code actually was negative during this period.

Finally, according to research conducted by James A. Mitchell, a fellow at the Center for Ethical Business Cultures, the organizations that build ethical cultures outperform those that do not. Mitchell's paper shows that ethical leadership adds substantial economic value to a corporation, "making the whole economic pie bigger" so that each of the key stakeholders—customers, employees, owners, and the community at large—can each receive a "bigger piece." Thus, in the longer term, the ethical corporation has a significant advantage over its competitors.[3]

STAKEHOLDER APPROACH

Stakeholders are an important part of any discussion of business ethics. Organizations large and small are webs of interdependencies. Shareholders, lenders, benefactors, customers, vendors, employees, trustees, directors, communities, and others gain from having organizations flourish. Each of these constituencies also suffer when the organization is weakened or ceases to exist, thus each has a stake in the successful outcome of the organization. A *stakeholder approach* to business has become very popular with those concerned with corporate social responsibility and a values-based business approach.

The stakeholder approach recognizes a basic fact: that the fate of an organization affects more than the owners of the business. It also recognizes the trust and goodwill that inures to the benefit of the organization when all stakeholders are valued. Further, as indicated earlier, studies have found a correlation between corporate social performance and financial performance.[4] The stakeholder approach has certainly gained traction as it is difficult to find major public companies, institutions of higher education, and nonprofits discussing results purely in terms or profits or grants. Rather, the discussion centers around "service." The following is from the General Electric (GE) Web site:

Responsible leadership and operational excellence are hallmarks of GE. Our citizenship framework—make money, make it ethically and make a difference—enables us to make contributions and create value for society in ways that are aligned to the business strategy of the company.[5]

From Duke University:

While Duke will continue to embrace the essential aspects of specialized research, teaching and learning, the university will build on its special strengths in collaboration and connection of knowledge to real-world problems. More than ever, we will prepare students to approach issues with creativity, flexibility and a curious mind. Engagement across lines of race, ethnicity, religion and national culture will become more important as training for an increasingly interconnected world.[6]

From the San Francisco Ballet:

The mission of San Francisco Ballet is to share the joy of dance with its community and around the globe . . .[7]

A dedication to broad social responsibility is becoming more a part of American organizations.

Proponents of this strategy view this as taking an *enterprise approach* to business. Ultimately, the enterprise approach means combining business thinking with values thinking to serve and integrate the interests of all stakeholders—in other words, an approach that considers the common good. This approach is well expressed in *Managing for Stakeholders: Survival, Reputation, and Success*.[8] The enterprise approach helps leaders to think about operations and processes in terms of how to create as much value as possible for all stakeholders, rather than the traditional view of distributing the burdens and benefits of corporate activities among them. The objective is to increase the pie, rather than dividing the spoils differently. The enterprise approach requires that ethical leaders have a sense of clarity around their values and what they stand for, and leadership must be engaged in conversations about how business can make society better. It requires that ethics and leadership go together. Leaders are found at all levels of an organization. When ethics and leadership go together, the result is honorable behavior for the individual, and collectively, the organization.

ALL ANIMALS ARE EQUAL, BUT . . .

While the pigs in Orwell's *Animal Farm* were unwittingly highlighting the hypocrisy of the elite, as more and more stakeholders enter the picture, it raises the question of prioritizing stakeholders. Are all stakeholders equal or are some more equal than others? Even with the notion of increasing the size of the pie, how are choices to be made? Reasonable people differ. Commented one private equity vice president:

> There is a very dangerous modern trend to hold the corporation . . . accountable to the "stakeholders." . . . Usually, this starts off as "shareholders plus employees" but often progresses to "shareholders plus employees plus community" and eventually to "shareholders plus employees plus general public." This ignores two key issues.
>
> First, corporations are simply no good at philanthropy. Nor should we want them to be . . .
>
> Second, assigning any responsibility to the corporation other than to make a profit for the shareholders (be that short term or long term) is very dangerous. By what standard do we measure this obligation? Is the corporation beholden to the employees to provide employment? To the community to provide tax revenue and gainful employment to its residents?[9]

Private equity companies usually own a substantial concentration of a firm's capital. That is, by the nature of being private, the ownership structure is spread among a few owners who are rightfully concerned about return on their invested capital. Further, private companies are not liquid and cannot easily be sold. It is understandable that, under these circumstances, business owners are insistent that business managers serve their needs first. In addition, the private company may be reliant on the owners for future capital. The willingness of current owners or new owners to inject capital into a private company is dependent on direct return to the owners, not whether the business is serving society in some general way.

Contrast this position with an owner of shares of GE. General Electric has approximately 10 billion shares outstanding. Its ownership is widely distributed with the largest shareholder owning only 3.3 percent.[10] Just over one-third of the shares are owned by 50 institutional investors, so each averaged approximately 73,000,000 shares or 0.7 percent of the company. Even so, in August 2008, the cost of being in the top 50 shareholders of GE was $2 billion.[11] GE is also very liquid for investors, with over 100 million shares trading hands on an average day. Given these circumstances, a holder of General Electric stock is not an "owner" in the same way as the private equity investor. The holder of GE sees their return through dividends and, more importantly, appreciation of the stock. The price of an established, liquid, global enterprise, such as GE, is derived from a variety of factors that will not play as important a role in determining return to the private equity investor.

Moving out of the corporate realm, universities offer a similar dilemma. Harvard University and Boston University (BU) are both private higher educational institutions in Boston, but the financial resources available to them are vastly different. At the beginning of 2008, Harvard endowment topped $34 billion. BU's endowment was just over $1 billion. Harvard University has an enrollment of approximately 20,000 undergraduates and graduates, while BU is home to nearly 30,000 undergraduates and graduates. Measured on a per student basis, Harvard's endowment is nearly 50 times the size of Boston University's. Both institutions seek to provide a superb education and environment for their students, but the disparity in financial resources necessitates different approaches. Should the respective stakeholders for these universities be the same and, more to the point, be looked at similarly? It would seem to make sense for Harvard and BU to view their stakeholders differently.

A TWO-WAY STREET

As we entered 2009, the economic stress the country is experiencing provides a test for the enterprise approach and just who is a stakeholder in the organization. A prime example is the public debate over a taxpayer-funded bailout of the Big Three automakers: General Motors, Ford, and Chrysler. The situation is summarized in *Wall Street Journal* opinion piece by Holman Jenkins, Jr. in which he states: "In the continuing battle over Detroit, UAW chief Ron Gettelfinger doesn't seem to get the picture. Let's help him. With shareholders virtually wiped out and debt holders taking a massive haircut, labor is the only stakeholder with anything left to lose."[12] At the time this op-ed appeared, the United Autoworkers Union has steadfastly refused any near-term concessions and described the terms of the loans to GM and Chrysler as "unfair" and "singling out workers."[13] For the immediate discussion, it is unimportant to debate the dollars and cents, but rather to ask the question as to whether or not being a "stakeholder" is a two-way street.

The American economy has grown steadily since 1983. In the 289 months from November 1983 until December 2007, the U.S. economy experienced only 16 months of recession. When overall value is increasing, the discussion of who enjoys the benefits is quite different than in a period where the overall pie in contracting. If one defines "stakeholder" to be a person or entity that enjoys the fruits of success *and* sacrifices during difficult times for the benefit of the organization, the stakeholder list drops considerably. When faced with an exhausting list of stakeholders, the obvious questions is "Who will be there for us if the going gets difficult?"

Now it is clear that at certain times one can pinpoint the cause of financial difficulties, such as poor management. Typically, there is a responsible party that should bear the brunt of the sacrifice. As we enter 2009, the general economic malaise will affect a broad swath of organizations that will become collateral damage. Indeed, much of the debate around public bailouts surrounds the notion of the prudent being forced to come to the rescue of the profligate and the moral hazard that develops. For these organizations, the future will clarify who are the true stakeholders in their organizations.

UNCLE SAM

A brief note on the role of the government as a stakeholder in the organization: The idea that the government is a stakeholder in your organization in its sole capacity as the state is a steaming pile of horse apples. Unless the government plays another role—customer, vendor, lender—its capacity restricts its ability to play the role of a true stakeholder. This is not to say that the relationship must be adversarial; it is just that the government plays a very unique role in a capitalistic society and that role is not necessarily to promote the interests of the organization, but to promote the interests of society. Many times these interests do not coincide. It should be noted that this is not the general view of those who believe in the enterprise approach. Suffice to say that when the Internal Revenue Service (IRS) and the Department of Justice takes an interest in your organization, they do not usually start the dialogue with "I'm from the government and I'm here to help."

TOWARD A WORKABLE MODEL

This chapter frames the assumption that is used throughout this book. It is important for each organization to take an enterprise approach to building value in its business. Value creation in a capitalist society is dependent on a variety of different players each of whom adds to the organization and plays a role. An organization must take care to identify "true" stakeholders in the organization, be they owners, shareholders, donors, students, employees, vendors, customers, communities, or any number of specific entities. A "true stakeholder" is a stakeholder who will participate in the success of the organization and can be called on to help the organization in difficult times. Entities that fit the first part of the definition, but not the second part of the definition are called "dependents." Not all stakeholders are created equal, nor are all equally important in times of crisis. Depending on circumstances, certain stakeholders may become more important during certain times then they would otherwise be. Finally, there are such things as transitional stakeholders or entities that may be true stakeholders for a short period of time. The media is a common example of what one might consider a transitional stakeholder. In each and every case, cultivating and enhancing stakeholder relations is crucial to the success of an organization and an important part of building an ethical environment or navigating an ethical challenge.

Building an ethical organization reaps greater rewards than simply preventing malfeasance. There is a direct correlation between the performance of companies built on a strong ethical foundation and superior performance in the marketplace. The benefits are not just a greater return to business owners, but also become apparent in brand recognition, sales, customer satisfaction and loyalty, employee productivity and satisfaction, and even reduced regulatory burdens. While we discuss tactical approaches to improving ethics and the ethical environment in your organization, it is assumed that the definition of your organization is broad enough to cover all true stakeholders. Active involvement of an organization's stakeholders in the creation of an ethical environment augments each of the initiatives the organization puts in place and further increases the chance of success.

■ NOTES

1. Thanks to Anjali Gupta for compiling the research.
2. Codes of ethics were loosely interpreted to include codes of conduct, governing principles, or other statements having the same purpose.
3. James A. Mitchell, *The Ethicial Advantage: Why Ethical Leadership Is Good Business* (Minneapolis: Center for Ethical Business Culture, 2001). Available from http://w–!>ww.cebcglobal.org/KnowledgeCenter/Publications/Ethical Leadership/TheEthicalAdvantage.pdf (accessed 19 January 2009).
4. M. Orlitzky, F. L. Schmidt, and S. L. Rynes, "Corporate Social and Financial Performance: A Meta-analysis," *Organization Studies* 24, no. 3 (2003): 403–441.

5. General Electric, "Citzenship," *GE.com*. Available from http://www.ge.com/company/citizenship/index.html (accessed 1 January 2009).

6. Duke Univeristy, "Making a Difference," *Strategic Plan*. Available from http://www.stratplan.duke.edu/ (accessed 1 January 2009).

7. San Francisco Ballet, "About," *SFBallet.org*. Available from http://www.sfballet.org/about/ (accessed 1 January 2009).

8. R. Edward Freeman, Jeffrey S., Harrison, and Andrew C. Wicks, *Managing for Stakeholders: Survival, Reputation, and Success* (New Haven: Yale University Press, 2007).

9. "From Shareholders to Stakeholders," *Going Private,* 16 June 2008. Available from http://equityprivate.typepad.com/ep/2008/06/from-shareholde.html (accessed 19 January 2009).

10. Figures derived from General Electric and other financial sources.

11. Even at the end of 2008 with prices depressed, the price of admission to this exclusive club was $1.2 billion.

12. Holman W. Jenkins, Jr., "Let Detroit Build Profitable Cars," *Wall Street Journal*, December 31, 2008, p. A7.

13. Press Release, United Auto Workers Union, UAW applauds auto loans, but says workers must not be singled out for unfair conditions. Available from http://www.uaw.org/auto/12_19_08auto1.cfm (accessed 19 January 2009).

CHAPTER 3

Why "Business" Ethics Is Not Just about Corporations

A lie can travel halfway around the world while the truth is putting on its shoes.

—MARK TWAIN

With the flow of information increasing each moment, an event can have an immediate and long-lasting impact on a business's reputation and how it is perceived in the marketplace. Organizations not classically considered "for-profit businesses" also rely on reputation and standing in their particular fields. Universities, professional firms, and nonprofits enjoy the economic and social benefits of a positive reputation as much as corporations. Lapses in ethics in corporations grab the headlines, but ethical lapses are hardly the exclusive purview of businesses. Academia, nonprofits, and, of course, government all face issues with ethics lapses.

While individual and group behavior is similar across organizations, there are many differences in the circumstances at noncorporate organizations that make resolution difficult. In a corporate entity, the power of management, in particular the ability to terminate employment of an individual, focuses responsibility and accountability at the top. But in noncorporate entities, power can be distributed in such a way to make centralized control difficult.

CASE STUDY   THE DUKE UNIVERSITY LACROSSE SCANDAL

BACKGROUND

Richard Brodhead was about as pure a Yale product as they come. He graduated from Yale College *summa cum laude* in 1968, received an M.A. from Yale in 1970, and received his Ph.D. in English from the Yale Graduate School in 1972. That year, Brodhead was appointed an assistant professor of English at Yale. In 1980, he received tenure and became a full professor and Dean of the English Department in 1985. A charismatic lecturer, he became Dean of Yale College in 1993.

Dean Brodhead's resume was impressive: He is the author or editor of more than a dozen books on American authors and received the William Clyde DeVane Medal for Outstanding Scholarship and Teaching from the Yale Chapter of Phi Beta Kappa. He had been a visiting professor at the École Normale Supérieure in Paris and had won several scholarly honors and fellowships, including Guggenheim, Woodrow Wilson, Danforth, and Morse fellowships. In 2002, he received an appointment to the J. William Fulbright Foreign Scholarship Board. While not without controversy, Richard Brodhead was, by all accounts, a superb scholar, professor, and dean.

Duke University traces its roots back to the founding of Trinity College in North Carolina in 1838. Almost 60 years later, Washington Duke offered a $100,000 endowment to Trinity, which was moved to Durham, North Carolina, with the stipulation that the college extend equal opportunity to women.[1] In 1924, Washington Duke's son, James Benjamin "Buck" Duke, established the Duke Endowment with a grant of $40 million to support the university and other worthy organizations in North and South Carolina. At that time, the institution changed its name to honor the elder Duke.[2]

In the mid-1980s, Duke University started to gain national prominence because of two men—one a professor of psychiatry and the other a West Point basketball player. Professor of psychiatry H. Keith H. Brodie was named president of Duke University in 1985. Shortly after his arrival, the Duke University men's basketball team, coached by a former West Point point guard named Mike Krzyzewski, reached the championship game of the NCAA tournament and became a fixture in NCAA basketball post-season play. President Brodie's development of Duke University as an academic force and Coach Krzyzewski's transformation of the Blue Devils basketball team into the face of Duke as a national sports power propelled Duke University into the top tier of universities in the country, routinely placing in the top 10 overall rankings. Once an excellent regional university, Duke is now a recognized high-quality international education and research institution.

President Brodie also sought to make Duke a welcoming place for minority faculty by initiating the Black Faculty Initiative. His efforts were accelerated and expanded under his successor, Nan Keohane, who added a Women's Initiative. Both programs sought to increase the number of minority and women professors at the university and was one of the first major university outreach programs announced. In the mid-1990s, many universities sought to expand minority and gender studies programs to introduce both a more diverse discussion on issues and to make campuses a more welcoming environment for minority faculty and, hopefully, students.[3] Duke University had an additional interest in reaching out to minorities in that the population of Durham is roughly evenly split between white and nonwhite minorities.[4] As in many universities, relations between the student and city residents were strained. In the case of Duke, however, there was added racial and social tension of a predominantly white, well-off student body and the blue-collar, minority local community.

(Continued)

On top of all these dynamics, one has to briefly discuss the notion of "tenure." In its simplest form, tenure is an employment contract whereby the professor is granted perpetual employment absent dismissal for "cause." Once received, tenure is a permanent job contract. Tenure is typically granted after some period of time and professors during this time are said to be on a tenure track. Not all professors are on a tenure track and not all tenure track professors are granted tenure, but tenure is the holy grail of the professorial profession. Standards for granting tenure vary, but are usually based on research, teaching, publication, service to the department or university, and student mentoring.

The reason for tenure is academic and scholarly freedom. Tenured professors are more likely to pursue subjects or topics that are less mainstream, but nonetheless important or of scholarly interest. Tenured professors do not fear retribution from the administration for unpopular views and are allowed a certain amount of economic freedom for the professor to invest time in a pursuit which may not produce immediate results. Thus, the tenured professor is free to do as he or she would wish without specific regard to its impact to the university. In other words, one of the unintended effects of tenure in the university system is to dissociate the apparent authority of the professors within the university system with the responsibility for the impact of their actions on the university and its community. This dissociation between authority to act and responsibility for consequences creates a difficult moral hazard and management challenge.

This mixture of personalities, good intentions, ambition, and academic tradition came into conflict when, on March 13, 2006, what started out as a typical party ended up in a perfect storm of race, class, and gender. While the details of the incident are unnecessary for our discussion, a general outline of the incident is in order. At an off-campus party attended primarily by the Duke men's lacrosse team, two strippers were hired to perform. They performed during a half-hour period and left the party. A course verbal exchange between an attendee and one of the dancers caused the show to be stopped. After almost leaving, the strippers reentered the house and went into the bathroom. Approximately 75 minutes after arriving, the dancers left the party and racial epithets were exchanged as they left the premises. Soon thereafter, one of the women alleged that she was raped by three of the attendees of the party.

The initial reaction of Duke University was concern, caution, and restraint. The athletic director forced the team to forfeit two lacrosse games due to the fact that underage drinking occurred at the party—a violation of university rules. Several days later, President Brodhead cancelled the remaining season. It was beginning to be clear that this was a major incident as 46 of the 47 lacrosse players were asked to submit DNA samples[5] to be tested against DNA found in the alleged victim. While no indictments had been issued at the time, the allegations stirred passions.

The tenor of the situation changed dramatically in early April, when a group of faculty published an advertisement in the *Duke Chronicle* entitled "What Does a Social Disaster Sound Like?" The authors claimed to be "listening" to students saying that racism and sexism were "part of the experience" at Duke. The group said they were "turning up the volume in a moment when some of the most vulnerable of us are being asked to quiet down while we wait. To the students speaking individually and the protestors making collective noise, thank you for not waiting and for making yourselves heard."[6] Issues of guilt or innocence, truth or fiction, and basic facts seemed to take a backseat to historical wrongs. As the ad said, what happened was "apparent . . . regardless of the results of the police investigation . . ." As one commenter noted, "[t]hat 88 faculty members—much less entire departments—would have signed on to such a document suggests that whatever plagues Duke's campus culture goes beyond the lacrosse team's conduct and the administration's insufficient

(*Continued*)

oversight of its athletic department."[7] Without a balancing voice from other professors, the Group of 88 became the voice of the faculty at Duke.

LEADERSHIP PERSPECTIVE

President Brodhead was no stranger to controversial campus situations, nor could he be unfamiliar with the challenges often posed with community relations. But he was relatively new to Duke University and the elms and ivy of New Haven, Connecticut, could not have prepared him for the historical racial tension in the South. Further, the deliberate fanning of race, gender, and class tensions in an already difficult situation seemed to be a deeply irresponsible move. While political activism among professors is not new, the drastic increase in liberal arts professors over the prior years drastically altered the blend of political views. For example, in 2004, a Duke Conservative Union study showed that the humanities department had 142 registered Democrats and eight registered Republicans.[8] While political affiliation may not have had any impact, it was certain that the faculty saw their role as political activists.

President Brodhead's initial reaction was to acknowledge the differing points of view and to urge everyone to wait for the results of the investigation. He was clearly concerned that so many of the faculty were involved in endorsing the advertisement. Just months before, Lawrence Summers had resigned as president of Harvard University after Summers's remarks about gender differences in the sciences provoked faculty outrage. Brodhead had every reason to be concerned.

This proved to be a mistake. It is unclear whether President Brodhead trusted those involved to act responsibly, was restrained by lawyers from speaking out, or did not have enough confidence to provide leadership, but in the critical first few days and weeks after the incident, the defensive posture of the administration further polarized the community. The damage control with the professors and the community encouraged a generalization of the problem. The question moved from guilt or innocence to being an example of historical clashes amongst race, gender, and class and as evidence of racism and sexism at Duke. The faculty found a receptive ear in the local and national news media that latched on to the conduct of the lacrosse players in hiring strippers as athletes gone wild. But the biggest tragedy was to come.

As one might expect, there was a tremendous deference to the ongoing investigation. The case was in the hands of the district attorney (DA) for Durham County, Michael Nifong. Interviews were conducted and DNA samples were taken to establish which players may have been involved in the rape. In early April, the results of the DNA testing indicated no DNA from the lacrosse players were found on or in the accuser. Further, the results of a photo line-up had established the identities of the alleged attackers. To the casual observer, justice seemed to be taking its course.

As we now know, the accusation was false[9] and the conduct of Nifong resulted in his disbarment and a brief jail sentence. The three accused players, as well of the rest of the team, were only guilty of loutish behavior and violation of university policies regarding underage drinking.[10] The impact of the accusations on the lives of the accused was severe: academically, emotionally, and financially. The impact on Duke was also serious and tension continues. At the heart of the criticism are President Brodhead and the administration of the university. But how fair is the criticism?

20/20 HINDSIGHT

As we discuss cases going forward, you will see some common ingredients throughout that are neatly illustrated by this situation. First, in an effort to be "fair," President Brodhead and Duke's administration treated all actors equally. Whether the crisis is a charge of rape or corporate fraud, the worst reaction is to be "evenhanded" in the face of damning evidence. In these situations, there will inevitably be interests that the organization's leadership must protect and parties that act against those interests. Sitting on the sidelines, which is what President Brodhead and the Duke administration seemed to do, demonstrates both weakness and a tacit acceptance of any behavior contrary to the interest of the organization. Further, the demonstration of weakness will only encourage further bad behavior.

Second, when crisis strikes, actors do not always behave ethically. The Duke lacrosse incident did not start as an ethical problem, but developed into one with the actions of the faculty and the district attorney. While the players were exonerated by the end of 2006, within 30 days of the party, there was ample reason to suspect the accusations were false. To many without a vested interest in the outcome, the innocence of the players and the unethical behavior of the DA were obvious by the end of May.[11] To be fair to the administration, the DA was equally clear that he thought a crime occurred. In the face of two extreme claims, the university tried to split the baby when what it should have done was to zealously protect the organization and its stakeholders.

Finally, Brodhead and the administration did not seem to understand whose interests they were tasked to protect. It would seem that the university's interests were first and foremost at issue here: The leadership of Duke had a duty to protect the organization. Next would be the interests of the students—the university's equivalent of "customers." While the idea of *in loco parentis* no longer strictly applies to universities, there is still a notion that the university should provide a protective environment for the students. In this case, the appearance of "fairness" looked to the student body as abandonment. The faculty presents a different problem. While the role of tenured faculty is unique to higher education, the moral hazard faced by the professors is common in all organizational settings.

Moral hazard in its broadest sense means that someone who is insulated from the consequences of their action will behave differently than someone who has to bear the risk. A more acute moral hazard occurs when someone can reap a tangible *reward* of an action while knowing someone else bears the cost. Moral hazard represents the most common ethical problem dealt with on a day-to-day basis. In its most common and "innocent" form, moral hazard occurs in an organization where authority is disassociated from responsibility. In the current case, the 88 faculty members carried authority by reason of their position, but had neither responsibility for action nor responsibility for the consequences of their accusations.[12] Taking the faculty at its word, their issue was the historical mistreatment of minorities, women, and the underclass; but the results of their actions were highly prejudicial to the accused and inflammatory for the community. Regardless of the intent, the faculty was seen as having authority within the university without consideration for the consequences to the university. This situation lay unaddressed by university leadership until months after the damage was done. Brodhead and the university administration implicitly bought into the notion that the lacrosse incident represented something larger, a statement on society or historical wrongs. It did not. The incident was not a symbol; it was an event of profound importance and impact to the accused lacrosse players and the university. By abstracting the problem, the university leadership lost control of the solution.

THE BURDEN OF EXPECTATIONS

Incidents of ethical lapses in noncorporate settings are no more or less common than in corporate settings. In many ways, though, the noncorporate world has greater challenges than the corporate world. In the corporate world, the pursuit of the profit motive seems to carry with it an expectation that a corporation will behave aggressively as they fulfill their fiduciary duty to their shareholders. At universities, in government, or at a nonprofit, there may be a greater public expectation of ethical behavior as these organizations' fiduciary duty is more akin to a public trust.

It is worth spending a few minutes on fiduciary duty. The notion of a *fiduciary* is from Roman law, that is, something of value is placed in care of one person for the ultimate benefit of another. We may think of a trustee of an estate being a fiduciary for the heirs of the estate; but the idea is that the fiduciary puts the interest of the beneficiary, generally called the *principal* or *entrustor*, before their own or the interests of others. The fiduciary relationship may extend to a single person, a group of people, or to any other legal entity, but in each case a fiduciary duty is said to encompass both a duty of loyalty and a duty of care.[13] The whole of the relationship is one based on trust as one might gather from the origin of the term *fiduciary*, which comes from the Latin *fiducia,* meaning "trust."

Not all business relationships are fiduciary ones, of course, and there is often confusion as to what constitutes a fiduciary duty. The general idea is that a fiduciary "stands in the shoes" of the entrustor with power over something of value that the entrustor has complete rights to. So there is a relationship of power and dependency. The fiduciary exercises power and the entrustor is completely dependent on the acts of the fiduciary. Circling back, as noted earlier, executives and the board of a corporation owe their duty to shareholders. Governing board trustees and university administrators have a fiduciary duty to the long-term interests of the institution.[14] Government leaders have a fiduciary duty to the public. For not-for-profits, the fiduciary duty extends to the objects of the organization. For a charitable not-for-profit, this duty extends to some of society's most vulnerable members. When that public trust is broken, the consequences are just as harsh.

CASE STUDY	THE UNITED WAY

"Charity has always begun in the hearts of the well-intentioned." For the United Way of America, the beginnings can be traced back to Denver, Colorado, in 1887 when Frances Wisebart Jacobs and other church leaders formed the Charity Organization Society. The initial purpose was to focus on the roots of poverty more than simply the giving of alms and look at social services as a way to self-sufficiency. As charities formed across the country, associations of charities were created to help coordinate these various groups. In addition to associated charities, community chests collected funds from businesses and distributed them to various community projects. As time progressed, many of these local charitable organizations "merged," to pool resources and ideas. By 1970, what was then known as the United Community Funds and Council of America changed its name to United Way of America. Today, the United Way is the largest charity in the United States, with approximately 1,300 local chapters.

Unfortunately, the United Way organization has for many years struggled with a spate of ethics scandals, ranging from financial mismanagement at local chapters to criminal convictions of senior leadership on a national level. In 1992, United Way president, William Aramony, and two other senior executives were found guilty of 25 counts of criminal behavior, including fraud, conspiracy, and money laundering; this incident, coupled with numerous fundraising and accounting scandals that emerged at local United Way chapters throughout the nation, brought into question not only general governance practices in the nonprofit sector, but also what constitutes ethical management of charities and how to bring about a greater level of accountability among leaders in the public sector.

While the United Way's receipts more than tripled during the 22 years of Aramony's tenure as president and CEO, coinciding with the increase in revenue were unprecedented raises in Aramony's salary and extravagant perks, including $20,000 in limousine expenditures in a single year. A $430,000 per year salary and lavish perks may not have seemed remarkable compensation for an executive whose policies tripled a company's revenues in the corporate world; however, in an organization fueled by donor contributions made to serve the needy, Aramony's compensation level and extravagant lifestyle seemed grossly inappropriate and a serious breach of public trust. When news of his salary and personal gains became public, donations to United Way declined dramatically at both the local and national level.

(Continued)

The Aramony scandal may have been the most notorious example of malfeasance at the United Way. However, the organization continues to face embarrassing and damaging exposures of financial mismanagement and corporate abuses at the local chapters. Most recently, the United Way chapter of the Central Carolinas generated controversy when the public learned that chapter president, Gloria Pace King, was receiving the highest salary and benefits package in the United Way system, including a retirement package of $450,000 to $500,000 per year through 2010. Public outrage prompted the agency's Board to replace the executive with a new CEO and a drastically reduced compensation package. Critics of the organization nonetheless fumed over the lack of transparency and oversight that enabled King to have been offered such an extravagant pay package.

ANALYSIS

Many attribute a general movement toward governance reforms in the nonprofit sector in the late 1990s directly to the series of United Way scandals that came to light during that decade. Since that time, certain legislative measures have been put in place that impacts the oversight of charitable organizations. For example, nonprofits must comply with many of the corporate governance provisions and disclosure requirements set forth in the Sarbanes-Oxley Act of 2002. Nonetheless, concern about ethical conduct and accountability in the nonprofit arena still remains high, as does the suspicion that nonprofits use their tax-exempt status to evade appropriate disclosure practices. A Harris poll in 2006 revealed that only 1 in 10 Americans believed that philanthropies operated in an "honest and ethical" manner. Supporting this skepticism, in his book, *Masters of Deception: The Worldwide White-Collar Crime Crisis and Ways to Protect Yourself* (John Wiley & Sons, 1996), Louis Mizell, Jr. devotes an entire chapter to chronicling "cheating charities," claiming that there is evidence that more than $21 billion is stolen by executives of American philanthropies every year.

A BROAD IMPACT

Ethics scandals in the nonprofit sector are frequently associated with weak leadership and poor governance, conditions that similarly plague the for-profit sector. However, the repercussions of ethics violations in the nonprofit world are, from a societal perspective, potentially more damaging than those in the corporate world. The mission of most nonprofits involves making positive social impact; clearly, incidents of fraud, corruption, and financial mismanagement undermine and detract from the beneficial social contribution made by such organizations. Ethical misconduct, furthermore, erodes donor confidence and the credibility of the organization, severely impeding the organization's ability to carry out its mission.

The United Way ethics scandals have been highly publicized and have so profoundly damaged the organization's reputation and the confidence of its donors that some watchers now question its ability to survive. Indeed, the organization is struggling to revive donor interest and regain its former fundraising prowess. However, the current president and CEO, Brian Gallagher, openly acknowledges the impact that the incidents of misconduct have had on the organization and has proposed measures, including the passage of the Standards of Excellence, a set of standards for financial reporting and accountability, to try to restore integrity to the organization.

The United Way enjoys a recognized brand and still holds many valuable affiliations, including a 35-year relationship with the National Football League. This relationship includes other major sponsors, such as the Home Depot. After a drastic decline in donations, the United Way has seen donations rebound, in particular with local chapters that were not implicated in the scandal. Further, the United Way and its chapters and affiliates earned recognition for aiding the victims of Hurricane Katrina, a big step in reminding the public of the good works the United Way performs.

All organizations struggle with providing an environment to foster ethical decision making, whether that organization is a for-profit business or a not-for-profit charity. And ethical lapses hurt *all* organizations, not just those looking to make a profit. Further, for those organizations depending on reputation or trying to develop a reputation, the consequences of ethical lapses go far beyond the bottom line to the heart of the organization.

◼ NOTES

1. While Trinity College was open to women since the Civil War, there were still many limitations on the ability of women to get full degrees.
2. Trinity remains the name of the undergraduate College of Arts and Sciences.
3. The term *minority*, as is commonly used in discussing academia, generally omits Asian students and faculty and focuses on blacks, Hispanics, and Native Americans.
4. Durham County, North Carolina, "Population Profile Durham County and the City of Durham," February 2005. Available from http://www.durhamnc.gov/departments/planning/pdf/demographics.pdf (accessed 20 January 2009).
5. The omitted team member was black and the accuser said the rapists were white.
6. "What Does a Social Disaster Sound Like?" *Duke Chronicle*, April 6, 2006.
7. K. C. Johnson, "Duke's Poisoned Campus Culture," *Insider Higher Ed*, May 1, 2006.
8. K. C. Johnson, "Duke Lacrosse and the Professions of Diversity," *Minding the Campus,* May 22, 2007.
9. It should be noted that the accuser has penned a memoir in which she maintains she was attacked, though the final investigation could find no DNA, medical, or witness accounts collaborating her story.
10. This statement should not be taken as an endorsement of the actions of the lacrosse players in any way nor is it meant to indicate that underage drinking or hiring of strippers is acceptable behavior for college students or anyone for that matter. It is merely to suggest that reaction was disproportionate to the offense.
11. In particular, one of the accused could demonstrate with testimony, ATM receipts, and a cell phone record that he was not at the party at the time of the alleged assault; exculpatory evidence the DA refused to consider.
12. For a comprehensive critique of the Duke lacrosse scandal, see Stuart Taylor, Jr. and K. C. Johnson, *Until Proven Innocent: Political Correctness and the Shameful Injustices of the Duke Lacrosse Rape Case* (New York: Thomas Dunne Books, 2007). For a defense of the faculty members, see "The Duke

Lacrosse Case: A Duke Professor Pens an Expose of KC Johnson," *Brian Lieter's Law School Reports*, December 19, 2007. Available from http://leiter lawschool.typepad.com/leiter/2007/12/the-duke-lacros.html (accessed 20 January 2009).

13. Tamar Frankel, "Fiduciary Duties," in *The New Palgrave Dictionary of Economics and the Law*, vol. 2, Peter Newman, ed. (London: Macmillan Reference Limited), pp. 127–128.

14. Aims C. McGuinness, Jr., "The Functions and Evolution of State Coordination and Governance in Postsecondary Education," in *State Postsecondary Education Structures Handbook* (Denver: Education Commission of the States, 1997).

CHAPTER 4

A Historical Review

Concordia res parvae crescunt. (In harmony small things grow.)

—Motto of the Brothers of Saint Francis Xavier

Ethics is often an uncomfortable topic for the simplest of reasons: We presume we are ethical individuals, but we do not want to probe deeply into the matter and possibly test that assumption. It is easy to say "Do the right thing." However, none of us are saints and the question of what we would do under pressure to compromise our values is not polite dinner conversation. But we do not have to be saints to appreciate, value, and live an ethical life. The idea of upstanding citizenship, morality, ethics, and fairness is so much a part of our lives that we forget how recently this was not the norm, and in how many places it still is not.

The evolution of ethics and how society views ethical behavior is instructive in a number of ways. First, the fact that behavior evolved in and of itself is instructive for leaders examining their organizations. As you will see, ethics does not just happen and will not happen without certain foundations being in place. Looking around us, the building in which you sit, the plane in which you fly, and your home are the result of some cooperative human endeavor. At some point in our

39

evolutionary past, humans may have tried to be solitary creatures, but that could not have lasted long. Humans formed groups and the co-operation between humans led to the advancement of mankind.

Groups, even groups of two, require an understanding of how to behave. The record of the first organization undermined by unethical behavior is lost in history, but one can imagine that Grug the Hunter was out on the Serengeti Plain with his friends trying to bring down a fresh gazelle and one of them decided to take a bit more than their fair share. This internal notion of "fair share" started the moment two humans first cooperated toward a common objective. So, broadly understood, ethics is a fundamental underpinning to any successful cooperative venture.

Think about your own close relationships. To take an example, spouses develop boundaries of what is unacceptable behavior. Such behavior varies between couples and even varies between relation-ships one individual may have. From the establishment of boundaries, there develops a sense of what is acceptable behavior or what consti-tutes standards of behavior.

THE ANCIENT WORLD

The deep history of ethics is rooted in the first laws. As any parent knows, molding the behavior of a child often means behavior correc-tions. As much as the child psychology books tell you that you should mold behavior with positive reinforcement, the stress and strain of the moment makes it simple to define the boundaries and then to take the time to show how to act appropriately. Similarly, the history of ethics begins with laws.

Possibly the most famous sets of rules are the Ten Commandments. Given to Moses on the top of Mount Sinai, the Ten Commandments are the foundations of Mosaic Law and the Judeo-Christian tradition. The Ten Commandments establish the basic relationship between man and God—(the first four commandments) and God's view of the relationship between mankind (the next six commandments).[1] It was not just the Ten Commandments that God put to Moses. Exodus contains further details of the dos and don'ts that established a common law for the Israelites. Beyond the Commandments, God proscribed laws dealing with numerous situations, ranging from the buying of servants[2] to forbidding the cooking of a young goat in its mother's milk.[3]

Other ancient codes followed a similar pattern; the Code of Ur-Nammu of ancient Sumer developed around 2100 BCE contained approximately 50 different prohibitions similar in nature to the laws passed down in Exodus. Like the laws passed down in Exodus, the Code of Ur–Nammu deals with many offenses "common" to the time and proscribed punishment ranging from monetary payment to death. Similarly, the Code of Hammurabi of ancient Babylon, developed around 1760 BCE, expanded the scope of the rules encompassing nearly 300 acts or situations. It is interesting to note that the ancient codes are not simply laws, though most of them follow the "if you commit this crime, you will receive this punishment" pattern. Each of these ancient codes combines proscriptive behavior as well as prescriptive behavior. They tell us "Thou shall not steal"[4] (proscriptive) as well as "Honor thy father and mother"[5] (prescriptive). Similarly, the Code of Hammurabi says that "If a son strikes his father, his hands shall be hewn off."[6] But the Code of Hammurabi also contains prices for services. Thus, "[i]f a physician shall heal the broken bone or diseased soft part of a man, the patient shall pay the physician five shekels in money."[7]

In these early texts, we find the first evolution of societal behavior from the purely proscriptive, which confines the action we take, to the establishment of common custom or etiquette. As empires grew, a common foundation of laws and customs were required so that people within the empire knew what constituted criminal and what constituted appropriate behavior. Early regional empires were fairly homogeneous: Sumer comprised the region bracketed by the Tigris and Euphrates Rivers throughout southern Mesopotamia in modern day Iraq. Ancient Babylonia included the Sumerian Empire and added territory in central Mesopotamia. These old Mesopotamian empires were composed of people who were similar in culture and daily experience. Other tribal groups, such as the Israelites, were united in culture and tradition.

As empires grew ever larger, leadership was faced with the challenge of incorporating different cultures into a common kingdom. By far, the most common method was the point of a sword, but there were notable exceptions that were very successful. Cyrus II of Persia founded the Achaemenid Dynasty around 550 BCE in modern Iran with the unification of the Persian and Median Empires. During his reign, Cyrus the Great conquered much of the Middle East and showed great tolerance for local customs. The Achaemenids governed the empire by using a local system of provinces run by governors (satraps) who were responsible for all local administration of financial and government matters. The local governors paid tribute to the King, but were otherwise independent.[8] Persia under the Achaemenids is considered the first great empire. It encompassed size, persistence, and influence.

Cyrus's benevolence did not just flow from his good graces, but evolved from his religious beliefs. At the core of the Persian culture was Zoroastrianism. Zoroastrianism was the first religion to promote monotheism, though it was not strictly monotheistic. At the core of Zoroastrianism was the struggle between good and evil and one fought evil by the active promotion of good deeds. The moral aspects of Zoroastrianism are critical because Zoroastrians believe humans play an active role in the universal conflict between good and evil. Thus, your life represents a series of moral choices that will promote good (*asha*) or evil (*druj*). With this in mind, it is not difficult to see that acting in a moral way was critical to Cyrus's world view. By doing so, he directly impacted the universal struggle and assisted God in this struggle. Cyrus's benevolence had wide-ranging effect: It is recorded in the Bible that Cyrus allowed the Jews in Babylon to return from exile and issued an edict to rebuild the Temple.[9] Cyrus's pious and benevolent ways were carried on through his successors, notably Darius, and the Achaemenid Dynasty lasted until 330 BCE.

Greek Citizens' Code

During this same period, at the edge of the Persian Empire, philosophers in ancient Greece considered and debated ethics and morality. In examining the commandments and codes, we looked at an approach that combined elements or proscriptive behavior (don'ts) with those of prescriptive behaviors (do's) establishing both the boundaries of behavior and certain accepted practices among the members of a society. Classical Greek ethics differs from the codes in that it starts with the question of what makes a person lead a "good life." That is, rather than defining good or bad through the prism of whether an action is good or bad, the Greek philosophers sought to define the characteristics of a "good person" and construct a set of acceptable standards of conduct around those characteristics.[10] To use a prior example, the Fifth Commandment tells you to honor your father and mother and, by doing so, you are pleasing God. The Greeks would ask, what about your cousin or your neighbor? Put differently, should we define the behavior to narrowly apply to one's parents or shall we say that treating all others in an honorable way is the correct virtue leading to a happy life? By focusing on the aspects of character that made for a happy life, the Greeks deemphasize the notion of vice, such as the envy proscribed in the Tenth Commandment, and view envy as less important than its opposing virtue—gratitude.[11]

In Homer's *Iliad* and other Greek works, seven virtues of an honorable person emerge. Honorable Greek citizens show prowess in battle. They can speak eloquently and convincingly. They have a strong duty to family and their community. They exhibit kindness to supplicants. They honor the gods. An honorable Greek shows loyalty to friends and fellow soldiers.[12] Finally, one must achieve recognition as an honorable warrior. This final quality is important as we link the historical development of ethical behavior to the practical implementation of an ethical culture in an organization. As distinct from the religious view of Judgment in the eyes of God, the Greeks believed that public recognition of behavior was critical to establishing the virtues of a citizen. There is a classic phrase in ethics that "character is

what you are in the dark,"[13] but the Greeks did not put much cre-
dence in keeping good behavior a secret from the rest of the
community.

MILITARY CODES

As a practical matter, it is perfectly normal for societies to operate on
a day-to-day basis without descending into ethical chaos. The vast
experience of human history is pretty mundane: Farmers planted
their crops, shepherds watched their flocks, fishermen tended their
nets, and children and the home were looked after. The switch from
goatherd to Web programmer over thousands of years changed the
daily task, not the objective: earn a living and provide for the family.
But the military is an area that turns the typical human experience on
its head. George Orwell said, "People sleep peaceably in their beds at
night only because rough men stand ready to do violence on their
behalf." In the United States in 2008, we have a professional, volun-
teer army, but throughout most of history, the majority of soldiers in
an army were conscripts—often pressed into service. The mainte-
nance of unit cohesion in the face of the enemy required commanders to understand motivation.

As noted earlier, the Greek code placed special emphasis on the
warrior and the honor of a noble warrior. In the military, the notion
of honor has a special place. The act of killing is universally con-
demned in civil society. Thus when society asks individual to kill on
its behalf, there is a tension that develops within those individuals.
The perception of society of those acts is of paramount importance to
both society and the warrior. In response, rules developed to govern
the conduct of the warrior both during war and when interacting
with society. The reasons for this are practical and psychological. The
practical reasons are that unit cohesion requires an understood standard of behavior. Further, in the heat of battle, each warrior must
trust the actions of the others. If trust in the unit is lost, so is the battle.

Psychologically, battle still involves the act of killing, which is ingrained in society and its members as an evil deed. As such, the

warrior must believe in the righteousness of his actions and in his profession as higher calling. The strict adherence to a code of honor during violence allows the warrior to justify his actions and to go against his nature instinct. In addition, despite a "monopoly of arms" that signifies a characteristic of statehood, it would not do the king well to have his armies roving the countryside manhandling the peasants. The trust of the civilian population in the military and the restraint of the warrior are critical for a functioning society.

While the notion of honor in war is a primary theme in the ancient world of the *Iliad,* it persists in the later cultures of Europe, Asia, North and South America, and, indeed, throughout the world. What is striking is not that they developed, but how common the themes are in different cultures. Antarah ibn-Shaddad al Absi, or Antar the Lion, was born in the middle of the sixth century to an Arab father and Ethiopian mother, and grew to be a poet and warrior without peer. Antar is considered by some to be the father of chivalric knighthood and merit, who rose from humble beginnings to marry an Arab princess. Beyond being a consummate warrior, Antar developed a far-reaching reputation for gallantry, kindness, and loyalty. The Arab warrior tradition, embodied by Antar and told through the recounting of his heroics, spread across Africa. In North Africa, the Moors developed a chivalric tradition among elite knights. When the Moors crossed the Straits of Gibraltar and conquered the Iberian peninsula, they came in contact with Christian Europe and the actions of the Moorish knights influenced the warriors of Charlemagne and Carolingian France.

In the Western tradition, "chivalry" is associated with the Christian knights of Europe. Chivalry as an embodiment of virtue formed during the end of the tenth century. While influenced by the heroic tradition, the Chivalric Code was formalized by the Catholic Church for a more pedestrian reason: the collapse of the Carolingian Empire resulted in warfare among the remaining feudal lords. During these skirmishes, noncombatants, notably the peasants and the clergy, suffered greatly as the warring knights did not limit their violence to the opposing forces. The Chivalric Code articulated seven primary attributes of a Christian Knight: courage, justice, mercy, devotion, nobleness, generosity, and hope. The development of the code of chivalry was successful in easing the violence against noncombatants, but it was the Crusades that popularized the concept in Christian Europe.[14]

Similarly, half a world away in Japan, *bushido*, or the Way of the Warrior, developed to guide the conduct of samurai. *Bushido* developed around the tenth century for a similar purpose as chivalry: to give a higher purpose to the warrior class. Like chivalry, *bushido* included seven primary virtues: courage, rectitude, benevolence, loyalty, sincerity, glory, and respect. Comparing the bushido virtues with the seven chivalric virtues, one notices that five of the seven are strikingly similar. Courage, justice/rectitude, mercy/benevolence, devotion/loyalty, and nobleness/sincerity are quite comparable in intention and effect. While it is easy to infer historical and proximate connection between the warriors of Greece, Arabia, the North African Moors, and the European Christians, it is harder to connect the development of a very similar code in prefeudal Japan. The natural human communication that takes place amongst neighbors—hostile or friendly—could easily account for the passage of virtues and values from ancient Greece to post-Carolingian Europe. It is less likely that this accounts for the emergence of common themes in Japan. More likely, there is something common about the human experience and the development of societies across the globe that fostered the development of warrior codes with common themes.

CARDINAL VIRTUES AND VICES

The development of social rules started with the establishment of limits of behavior, moving quickly to the establishment of customs. The idea that there is a standard of behavior higher than that of custom—acting with honor—was introduced to society through the warrior code for several purposes, including unit cohesion and trust as well as for trust between the military—either a standing army or ready militia—and the civilian populace. While it makes sense for an honor code to be *imposed* on a military unit, the fact that it was also *adopted* voluntarily shows that groups with a common purpose and common practice are receptive to higher standards.

Standards of behavior were also very important to other groups as they emerged. Christian religious authorities were interested in mustering the faithful. As mentioned earlier, organized religion's primary domain is the relationship between its followers and God, but religion has also been concerned with relationships among the flock.[15] Christianity adopted the Cardinal Virtues as the foundation of a moral existence. Based on Plato's virtues and articulated by St. Thomas Aquinas in the *Summa Theologica,* the Cardinal Virtues are prudence, temperance, justice, and fortitude.[16] These virtues were "cardinal" because they formed the foundation of a moral life for all mankind. More than an ideal, the virtues set a standard of behavior for the clergy and missionaries that would soon begin to roam the world. Further, these standards formed the expectations of Christian behavior for all the faithful. A farmer, who could not achieve nobility by birth, could achieve nobility in the eyes of his community through virtuous actions and deeds.

BUSINESS ETHICS IN TIMES PAST

One of the effects of the establishment of large empires, such as the Persian Empire and, later, the Greek Conquests under Alexander and the Roman Empire, was the establishment of trade routes. The Silk Road emerged over history as several trade routes that were joined together. The Royal Persian Road was established and protected by the Persian Empire. The city of Alexandria, named after Alexander the Great, formed a crucial trade branch in north and east Africa and was watched over by the Egyptian empire ruled by Ptolemy and his line of successors, ending with Cleopatra. Later, the travels of Marco Polo were made possible by the Mongol Conquest of Asia and the reestablishment of the Silk Road. The Silk Road was in operation for approximately 2,000 years, though not continuously, due to war and conquest by unfriendly powers. The importance of trade between the near and far east, Asia, and Europe should not be underestimated and the closing of trade routes had a very large impact on the nobility. It was, of course, the Ottoman conquest of Constantinople that made the Genoese navigator Christopher Columbus's idea of a trade route to Asia across the Atlantic worth backing by the Queen of Spain.

TIMBUKTU

Some people are surprised to learn that Timbuktu is a real place. Located in Mali, Timbuktu was a major trading post in West Africa for the trans-Saharan caravan trade. Goods and salt were brought there from the north and traded for gold from southern Africa. As Islam spread, no less than three major Islamic universities were established in Timbuktu, including the famed University of Sankore. At its apex during the fourteenth century, the system of universities in Timbuktu was reputed to host 25,000 scholars and the city was home to 100,000 residents. Timbuktu became as important as any center of Islamic learning in the world.

Timbuktu owes its existence to the ethics of one woman. During the late eleventh century, the Tuareg tribe roamed the area around the Niger River looking for lands for their livestock to graze. During the dry season, the stagnant river was infested with insects, so a woman named Buktu dug a well and established a camp away from the Niger and its pestilence. Over time, Buktu developed a reputation for honesty, and tribesmen and traders would leave their goods in Buktu's possession for safekeeping during grazing or when the rainy season made carrying items difficult. Soon Timbuktu, or Buktu's Well, became a major trading post along the caravan route.

Trading offered profit for those hearty enough to bear the risks of transporting goods and as trade increased the merchant class. Successful trading allowed the establishment of a merchant class. Once again, the establishment of a group with a common purpose and common practices allowed the development of rules, customs, and higher standards.

For the European merchant class, one of the first influential writers on standards of business conduct was Saint Thomas Aquinas. Thomas Aquinas was born in 1225 in Sicily. As the younger son of a noble family, he was expected, at an early age, to be destined for the clergy.[17] Despite his family's deep ties to the Benedictine Order, Thomas—quite scandalously—was attracted to the Dominican Order. His family was so distraught that his brothers were sent to capture Thomas on the road and he was held captive by his family for two years. At the strong suggestion of Pope Innocent IV and the Holy Roman Emperor Frederick II, Aquinas was allowed to join the Dominicans.

Saint Thomas Aquinas's seminal work, *Summa Theologica,* is a compilation of Catholic teachings at the time. It is structured as a series of questions aggregated in parts relating to overall topics. It is impressive in its scope and uses as its logical base the arguments of a very broad selection of great thinkers. Aquinas cites not only Aristotle, but Arabic writers, Islamic theologians, and rabbinic scholars. In the Second Part, Aquinas addresses ethics and, in particular, addresses business ethics,[18] saying that it is unlawful to sell an item for more than it is worth. Further, Aquinas tells us that it is unlawful for a seller to sell defective merchandise and should make restitution if he does so. If there is a defect in the items that is known by the seller, the defect must be told to the buyer. Aquinas says it is lawful to make a profit, but it is unlawful to charge interest for a loan,[19] which he likened to thievery.

Yet Aquinas was not dogmatic and it would be remiss not to give credit to Aquinas for his appreciation for how the market worked. In his discussion about what is a "fault" in the merchandise, St. Thomas acknowledges three very important things about the market in his discussions. First, Aquinas acknowledges that the two of the same items may be of different quality and therefore may command a

(Continued)

different price. Second, local market conditions affect the price and he states a fair price gives "due consideration for conditions of place and time."[20] Finally, each buyer may value something differently because of its "usefulness" to the buyer, so the price may fluctuate from buyer to buyer. In summary, Aquinas felt that gain through the trade of goods was proper, so long as the trade was honest and transparent and that a merchant could set any price, so long as it was fair under the circumstances—not at all bad for a humble thirteenth-century friar.

CASE STUDY   ARTHUR ANDERSEN

It is no small irony that Arthur Andersen & Company no longer exists due to one of the largest frauds in the history of business. Arthur Andersen himself epitomized business ethics during the early part of the twentieth century. Born in 1885 to Norwegian immigrants, Andersen was orphaned at the age of 16. In 1901, he joined Fraser & Chalmers (later Allis-Chalmers) in the mailroom, but moved over to the accounting department. After brief stints at Price Waterhouse & Co. and Schlitz Brewing Company, he and a partner formed what would become Arthur Andersen & Co. in 1913, where he was senior partner until his death in 1947.

Arthur Andersen's values led the company for over 50 years. His basic maxim was "think straight and talk straight," and Andersen developed a reputation for honesty and integrity. He displayed no tolerance for clients who were not transparent in their disclosures. Faced with a client who was unhappy about the firm's treatment of costs, Andersen is reputed to have said, "There is not enough money in the whole of Chicago to induce me to change that report." In another incident, a steamship company seeking investors wanted Andersen & Co. to certify a report that dated prior to a major loss of a ship. While the numbers were accurate, Andersen refused to sign the report unless the event was disclosed.

His devotion to integrity was a major factor in his success.[21] Andersen stated in 1932, "If the confidence of the public in the integrity of accountants' reports is shaken, their value is gone. To preserve the integrity of his reports, the accountant must insist upon absolute independence of judgment and action. The necessity of preserving this position of independence indicates certain standards of conduct."

Andersen was also a firm believer in the accountant as a business partner and not simply a bean counter. As such, he set up the first consulting operation in 1918. This put him in sharp contrast with fellow accountants, such as George O. May at Price Waterhouse & Co., who felt fidelity to the profession required the profession to focus on accounting, audit, and tax only. Andersen felt that any conflict could be contained by his guiding principles: honesty and integrity, the one firm–one voice partnership, and extensive training in a common methodology.[22] Arthur Andersen did not care; he would do it his way.

While Andersen was honest, ethical, hard working, and built the firm with those who reflected his values and determination, he could be personally very difficult and estranged his original partner and brother due to business disputes. When Andersen passed away in 1947, he was succeeded by Leonard Spacek, another ethical leader and strong proponent of the professional responsibilities of accountants. Spacek continued to build Arthur Andersen & Co.'s reputation for integrity. Andersen and Spacek led the firm and the industry in promoting an ethical approach to the presentation of financial statements to the outside world. As stated earlier, it is no small irony that it was the massive fraud of one of their clients that led to the firm's downfall.

THE NATURE OF MAN

Thus far we have focused on the evolution of groups and behaviors. Groups evolve from the establishment of basic rules governing prohibited behavior to the establishment of generally accepted standards of behavior or customs. Finally, with groups that exhibit a strong common purpose and common practices, one can see the development of higher standards of behavior that can make the honorable members of the group. The vast majority of human behavior occurs in that second stage. Most people go through their daily lives at home and at work doing what is expected of them and nothing more or less. This is not an indictment as much as a comment on an average day. Yet watching how we behave in our day-to-day rituals and seeing both the occasional hero and occasional villain, it causes one to wonder what lies at the heart of each of us.

From the study of morality and ethics emerged a discussion of whether these qualities are innate. That is, what drives the behavior of any one person? Is there a change in man when he walks in from the wilderness and joins society? Is there an inherent conflict between man as an individual and man as a member of a group? For our purposes, though, the understanding of the evolution of thought as man entered society sheds light on how employees adapt to a corporate environment.

While the great early philosophers, such as Socrates, Confucius, and Aristotle, pondered the nature of ethics and morality, later philosophers delved deeply into the "true" nature of man. To put it another way, the early thinkers concerned themselves with the *end point* of a moral existence, while later thinkers, led by Thomas Hobbes, pondered where it started from. What is man in a state of nature? This is a critical question in our discussion because the challenge man felt initially entering into societies is only slightly less daunting than new employees feel entering into your organization. That new employee will react and adapt in similar ways as his or her ancient ancestors.

While not trying to relive those sociology classes, it might be beneficial to review some of the major lines of thinking. This is not meant to be an exhaustive discussion, so it necessitates a level of summarization that will not quite do justice to the philosophers. In the modern era, Thomas Hobbes is famous for saying that man in a state of nature lives a life that is "solitary, poor, nasty, brutish, and short."[23]

Hobbes saw the life of man as a perpetual battle of self preservation. War was the rule rather than the exception and man formed society under a strong authoritarian leader to escape his natural state.

John Locke had a more positive outlook on the nature of man. Locke believed man was inherently good and that there was a natural law based on reason derived from experience. Locke also believed that man assembled in society for the betterment of all, but did not see the natural state as war, but as independence and tolerance. Later, Jean-Jacques Rousseau popularized the concept of the social contract and saw government as a pure democracy. Rousseau did not believe in a representative system, such as parliament. Rousseau famously said men are "born free; and everywhere he is in chains."[24] Rousseau saw man as neither good nor evil, but in the absence of influence, do not seek to do each other harm. Further, as with any contract, Rousseau felt that man could leave the contract with society and become as free as when he was born.

At the heart of these philosophies is the notion of the social contract. The social contract between society and the individual demands that we, as individuals, give up certain freedoms in exchange for the benefits of society, most commonly framed in terms of protection. Thus, we restrict our rights in exchange for all the other members of society restricting theirs. While the philosophers frame the discussion in political terms, we can substitute any organization and apply the thinking as well. Under a Hobbesian view, we can well imagine a very strong CEO and a strict governance environment to keep those thieving employees in line.

Despite the amount of brain power dedicated to these questions, it is clear that no single answer became apparent. The debate largely focuses on the general state of man before entering society, but individuals are far more complex. Furthermore, psychology, that is, the study of human behavior, was not a formal discipline until the late nineteenth century through the work of Wilhelm Wundt, William James, and Sigmund Freud. The early and mid-twentieth century offered insight into what drives human behavior. While the early philosophers touched on the individual psychological aspects of man, twentieth-century philosopher Ayn Rand, as part of her philosophy of Objectivism, sees ethics through the prism of rational egoism. *Rational egoism* proposes that it is rational and moral to act in one's own self-interest. Rand brings her philosophy back to Aristotle and sees the pursuit of one's happiness as inherently moral. Rand did not believe in altruism.

But people can be altruistic. Each of these philosophies seems to suffer from a very narrow view of the complexity of the human psyche and what actually makes us happy. Humans react differently based on different circumstances. For example, imagine you are in college and there is a math test scheduled the next day. You go to the professor's office and turn the corner just to see him leave. As he goes, a few papers fall out silently to the floor. As the professor walks out of sight, you pick up the papers and recognize them as tomorrow's math test. Looking around, the hall is empty.

Now we all know what you should do, but guessing what you will do is very difficult. Suppose your grade to date is an "A." Suppose it is a "C." Suppose math is an elective. Suppose it is your major. Suppose the test comprises 5 percent of your grade. Suppose it comprises 50 percent. Combining these questions, the answer might be different if you are a math major with a "C" average and the test is 50 percent of your grade as opposed to being a philosophy major with an "A" average to date and knowing this is only 5 percent of your grade. Your decision might be different because each of these circumstances has a very different impact on your life. The "right thing" may be the same in all cases, but the burdens are not.

To take the example one step further, suppose there are three students who find the test. Faced with a choice to do right or wrong, what will the group decide? Will the math major with a "C" average lead the decision or the philosophy major with the "A"? We know how we should act under these circumstances, so why would we do differently? The years following World War II saw increasing research into moral behavior, and research found that, much like cognition, human's morality matures as we grow older. This research began to lead to an understanding of why the student would choose one option over the other. The 1960s saw major strides in understanding criminal behavior and the role of peer and other groups as a major influence on what choice is made. The result is a far greater understanding of the complexity of the student's decision and a more proper understanding of how to influence his decision to be the right one.

As executives and leaders, we must understand that "should" is not "will," and we need to be conscious of the circumstances. More to the point, we need to focus on creating environments that both minimize the chances that the test is dropped in the hall and maximize the chances that the employee will do the right thing.

That is what we will discuss next in Chapter 5.

NOTES

1. It should be noted for historical accuracy that Judaism and Christianity actually view the commandments slightly differently. Further, within Christianity, there are differences in the way the Ten Commandments are broken down. These distinctions revolve around the separation of the first two prohibitions (relating to the declaration of the One True God and the prohibition of false idols) and the final two prohibitions (relating to covetousness). Christianity also "moved" the Lord's Day from the Seventh Day (Sabbath or Saturday) to the First Day (Sunday). So it would seem that there is wiggle room even in God's laws.
2. Exodus 21:1.
3. Exodus 23:19.
4. *Ibid.*, 20:15.
5. *Ibid.*, 20:12.
6. Code of Hammurabi, § 195.
7. *Ibid.*, § 221.
8. But not completely: The satraps' CFO and the head of the local army both reported to the King directly.
9. Ezra 1:1,2.
10. Greek philosophers were interested in the notion of a virtuous society as well as a virtuous person. For our purposes, we are focusing on the Aristotelian notion of *eudaimonism,* or individual happiness.
11. I would note that according to Christian tradition, the opposing virtue of the vice "envy" is "kindness." In this instance, I define envy as the pain

suffered when one does not have something someone does. Envy empha-
sizes the position of need. Rephrasing this to form an opposite statement,
one comes to: the joy in appreciating what you have that others do not.
Using this definition, "gratitude" fits better than "kindness."

12. Athenian citizenship was limited to males who had completed military
training.

13. This phrase, or a variation of it, has been attributable to several people. The
earliest source is the evangelist D. L. Moody in the late twentieth century.

14. Chivalry also plays a prominent role in Arthurian legend. While Arthur as a
historical figure is described in writings as early as the ninth century, his
popular association with the Knights of the Round Table comes from Sir
Thomas Malory's *Le Morte d'Arthur,* written in the fifteenth century.

15. We should note that this is distinct from the relationships with other different faiths. That is a very different story.

16. St. Thomas Aquinas, *Summa Theologica*, First Part of the Second Part,
Question 61.

17. For the younger males of the Christian nobility, the clergy offered an
acceptable alternative since they did not stand to inherit family wealth or
titles.

18. St. Thomas Aquinas, *Summa Theologica*, Second Part of the Second Part,
Question 77.

19. *Ibid.*, Question 78.

20. *Ibid.*, Question 77, Article 2, Reply to Objection 2.

21. In particular, Andersen was the choice of firms who were looking to buy
another company. Strangely, Arthur Andersen was not popular with sellers.

22. Susan E. Squires, Cynthia J. Smith, Lorna McDougall, and William R.
Yeack., *Inside Arthur Andersen: Shifting Values, Unexpected Consequences*
(Upper Saddle River, NJ: Prentice Hall/Financial Times Press, 2003),
p. 38.

23. Thomas Hobbes, *Leviathan*, Part I—Of Man, Chapter XIII, Para. 9.

24. Jean-Jacques Rousseau, *The Social Contract, or Principles of Political Right*,
Book I, Chapter 1: The Subject of First Book.

CHAPTER 5

Why Do People Behave Badly?

What is left when honor is lost?

—PUBLILIUS SYRUS

MORAL DEVELOPMENT

Sad to say, but it is not very difficult to find ethical lapses. Even the most casual observer will not find it hard to find reports of embezzlement, sexual harassment, or other types of corporate fraud or malfeasance to the point where bad behavior seems to be a natural part of corporate life. Most times the damage is slight and the perpetrator is discovered and punished, but in many cases the damages are long lasting and severe. The tragedy here is not simply the bankruptcy of the company, but the potential loss of savings for hundreds or thousands who put their trust in management and the board. Malfeasance has existed since the days of Cain and Abel, but for organizational leaders and the stakeholders who put their trust in them, it must be managed and minimized. To do so requires an understanding of certain behavioral aspects of individuals.

Most people have enough experience with right and wrong to understand there is at least some temptation to behave badly. We see it in coworkers, friends, our kids, and, most personally, ourselves.[1] Using the company's postage meter is wrong, but not to the degree of embezzlement. Most of the bad behavior is quiet noise in the grand scheme of things, so situations like the fraud at Enron can still shock us. To be absolutely clear, these statements are not meant to justify any sort of unethical behavior, small or large, nor are they meant to imply that it is "okay" to snag office supplies once in a while. What should be noted is that there is a large psychological difference between the extremes, and we are focused on unethical behavior that can have a large, negative impact on an organization both financially and culturally.

As we saw in our brief look at history, there is a natural moral compass in humans. In an effort to understand qualitative differences in small acts and large, we look at basic psychological models in order to construct a workable framework for our purposes. For example, the moral development of an individual is critical in understanding behavior. Beginning in 1958, Lawrence Kohlberg outlined stages of moral development that people pass through as they mature and, in some cases, regress as they age. Based on Jean Piaget's pioneering work in cognitive development, Kohlberg outlined six stages comprising three levels of moral evolution and these levels give us a framework to judge moral maturity.

We will also look at Abraham Maslow's hierarchy focusing on "safety needs" as motivation for misbehavior. The psychological context is significant. As one reads about, say, Mark Whitacre, former president of Archer Daniels Midland's BioProducts division, convicted of price fixing and fraud, and Barry Minkow, the founder of ZZZZ Best carpet cleaners, convicted of racketeering, securities fraud, and embezzlement, the question that most often comes to mind is "What were they thinking?"

FRAUD TRIANGLE

There is plenty of literature on "what they were thinking," but what they were thinking is only part of the problem. One of the most common ways used to describe the conditions of unethical behavior is based on three elements commonly referred to as the *Fraud Triangle*. The Fraud Triangle describes the circumstances necessary for malfeasance to occur. It does not *guarantee* that malfeasance will occur, but the combination of these circumstances is a red flag.

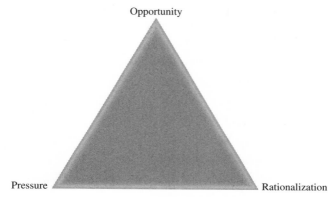

The Fraud Triangle

The first element is *opportunity*, which we address in Chapter 6. Opportunity simply means that the environment is such that malfeasance can occur. While there is simply no way in any organization to eliminate opportunity for malfeasance, there are ways to reduce the size of the opportunity available to an employee. Furthermore, by creating circumstances that counter such opportunities or create checks in the system to catch malfeasance, organizations can severely limit opportunities for malfeasance.

Pressure, the second element, is the trigger that causes bad behavior. Pressure can be caused by an individual need, group dynamics, or a combination of both. It is best to think of pressure as the environment around the decision-making process. In Chapter 6, we look at small group and large group dynamics; here, we confine the discussion to the pressure on an individual to commit a wrongdoing. The last element, *rationalization,* is the underlying thought process that makes good people justify bad behavior. Ultimately, rationalization is the core of the decision-making process when it is time for a "go" or "no go" choice to be reached. While individual rationalization is highly personal, it is also addressable by the organization.

It becomes immediately apparent what is *not* part of the Fraud Tri-angle: consequences. Put another way, misconduct or fraud is nearly always a result of shallow, short-term thinking. It also results from a lack of appreciation or understanding of the consequences the actions will have on the individual, his (or her) family, his coworkers, and the company. If those consequences were more fully understood, it would follow that malfeasance would be drastically reduced.

The final component in an individual's puzzle is history. An employee arrives in your organization with years of experiences be-hind him. His moral development is complete or nearly so. The vast majority of individuals will have developed patterns of behavior that repeat throughout their lives as similar circumstances arise. These pat-terns can indicate those people who are of higher risk of wrongdoing than others. Furthermore, personality traits that manifest themselves in ways that are otherwise lawful are often present in cases of organi-zational malfeasance. While the discussion revolves around ethics, there is no easy way to avoid the fact that corporate fraud is criminal behavior. While the circumstances may be different, the psychology of corporate wrongdoing is the same as criminal psychology and is illustrative of why white collar criminals commit crimes.

In summary, we can look at the moral development of an individ-ual to gauge the stage or sphere of *moral maturity*. The level of moral maturity determines the propensity of bad behavior and provides the basic decision-making framework for the life of an individual. Within this framework, absence of basic needs as articulated by Maslow create the particular stress or pressure point that triggers the bad behavior, especially in individuals with low moral maturity.

PROPENSITY

As discussed in Chapter 4, development of thought surrounding moral behavior has evolved as our experiences have changed and our understanding of psychology and biology grew. The interactions between individuals and society in feudal Europe or Japan in 1000 CE are quite a bit different than in Paris or in Tokyo in 2008. Where in the past people came together in groups for mutual defense or for social reasons, the advent of large cities and organizations brought people together for less critical reasons.[2] The ability to observe human interaction under "normal" conditions allowed the development of a new theory of social interaction and behavior. As mentioned, advances in understanding about the psychology and biology of behavior have led us to a point where general understanding of human psychology and behavior can help leadership bring out the best in an organization and limit the exposure of unethical behavior.

Can you imagine Mother Theresa embezzling? Mohandas Gandhi? Probably not. How about Jack the Ripper? While famous for another crime, it does not take a huge leap to believe him capable of embezzlement. There is a general human propensity for similar behavior patterns, especially with regard to questions of morality, ethics, and right and wrong. This propensity for consistent moral action is explained by the work of Lawrence Kohlberg of the University of Chicago.

Kohlberg's theory sees an individual's moral development evolving through six distinct moral stages. Attaining moral capacity in each subsequent stage allows an individual to more easily address ethical issues or dilemmas. Kohlberg's theories are based on Jean Piaget's work on cognitive development in children. Kohlberg found that Piaget's cognitive model worked well to frame moral development and observed how children of various ages worked out moral dilemmas. Another important factor is that Kohlberg saw moral development as universal and encompassing universal values. Thus, the model is based on moral reasoning and rejects moral relativism. This approach is important because a consistent behavioral standard throughout an organization is one of the critical features of a well-functioning company.[3]

For our purposes, a simplified approach to Kohlberg's methodology is adequate for an understanding of what drives individuals to make ethical choices. The framework for this decision making can be described generally by the notions of self, social, and societal. The *self sphere* focuses on the individual's own needs at the expense of others.

It is selfishness as a way of life and further assumes that others act in a like manner. A person whose moral development resides on the self sphere is a "me first" person. While this does not mean that others will not factor into the decision-making process, it does mean that they will only to the extent it will help the decision maker.

The *social sphere* focuses on the individual and a companion or other person in direct interaction with the individual. The interaction or connection may not be contemporaneous, but it is mutual. Being accepted or being liked becomes important. A person residing in the social sphere is conscious how decisions affect others and add that calculus in the moral decision-making equation. Again, individual interests play a part, but the effect on others plays a major role.

The *societal sphere* is a broad social construct encompassing not only the individual and companions, but third parties not within the immediate frame of reference, whether time, distance, or both. Achieving the greatest good for as many people as possible is the objective. A person in the social sphere is able to factor in all considerations and properly balance them for an objective decision.

As you can see, while Kohlberg describes these as levels to achieve, it is better for our immediate purposes to see these as spheres of moral engagement, in which each sphere represents the core of the next sphere and every person will have spheres of varying thickness or depth. According to Kohlberg, and very important for our purposes, you cannot progress from one sphere of moral engagement to the next without mastery of the current sphere. Thus, each sphere of engagement is a necessary prerequisite for the subsequent sphere. Further, according to Kohlberg, there is no regression once someone attains a certain sphere of moral engagement. As one might imagine, most people operate at a Social Level in the second sphere, which in Kohlberg's model was described as "conventional morality."

It is clear that while most people operate at the social sphere, most people react differently to ethical dilemmas. Criminal psychologists often speak of "propensity" and "events." *Propensity*, of course, is the natural inclination or tendency of an individual toward an action, while the *event* is the specific trigger or circumstances. The individual who resides on a higher sphere of moral development is more able to reason through an ethical dilemma than someone on a lower sphere. These people have a lower propensity to commit unethical acts and will continue to have a lower propensity throughout their lives. Yet our own experience tells us that people can do seemingly foolish things out of the blue. Are there influences that might—temporarily—increase the likelihood of unethical behavior?

Hierarchy of Needs

The answer is yes and brings us to the second area of psychology. In 1943, Abraham Maslow described a hierarchy of human needs.[4] This hierarchy, often depicted as a pyramid, is useful in that it matches what we see in normal everyday behavior. The five levels of the hierarchy are *physiological needs*, such as eating and sleeping; *safety needs*, such as personal and financial security; *social needs*, such as friendship and love; *esteem needs*, such as confidence and respect; and finally, *self-actualization*, which can be thought of as true harmony of a person's needs and wants.

Maslow's hierarchy differs from Kohlberg's stages of moral development in that Maslow's needs are instinctual, while Kohlberg's moral engagement requires reasoning to produce an outcome. Furthermore, while Maslow described successive needs as building on the fulfillment of basic needs, unlike Kohlberg, Maslow's theory allowed for a deprivation of needs. That is circumstances can change, even drastically, which would lead an individual to address the needs deficiency.[5]

The psychological connection between the level of moral maturity and Maslow's needs is the element of self-awareness. Self-awareness, in this framework, is the level of adherence to your moral maturity in the face of a crisis. The higher the level of self-awareness, the more resistant to unethical or questionable behavior the person will be—and a more self-aware person can reason through needs deprivation.

Conversely, if a person does not have a high level of self-awareness, the more likely he or she will be to respond to pressures in a way adverse to their interest. High self-awareness—a psychological trait—in the face of an ethical dilemma allows the individual to exercise the self-control—a behavioral trait—necessary to avoid the wrong decision. The bridge of self-awareness and self-control—that is, the sphere of moral maturity that provides the foundation for ethical decision making and the deficiency of a basic human need that triggers a behavior—goes a long way in explaining why good people do bad things.

CASE STUDY   WALT PAVLO [6]

Microwave Communications, Inc. (MCI) was founded in 1963 as a radio communications firm targeted at the trucking industry. After initially setting up a microwave communication station between Chicago and St. Louis, MCI sought to expand the system nationwide and grew quickly by buying out regional communications companies. By the late 1960s, MCI was a large enough force in the telecommunications market to compete head-to-head against the world's largest telephone company.

At the time, the telecom industry was a government-supported monopoly run by American Telephone & Telegraph Company (AT&T). "Ma Bell," as it was known, traces its roots back to the Bell Telephone Company, which was founded by Alexander Graham Bell's father-in-law and benefactor, Gardiner Greene Hubbard. AT&T began laying long-distance lines in the 1880s and its initial success gave it the wherewithal to buy up regional competitors if and when such competitors became threats or AT&T wanted to enter a new market. By 1892, the northeast was connected to Chicago, and by 1915, telephone lines reached across the country. Around that time, antitrust regulators began to get concerned about the size and power of AT&T, but also wanted to allow aggressive expansion of telephones across the country. This led to a "compromise" known as the

"Kingsbury Commitment," which, in 1913, set out the terms of the competitive landscape in the telephone industry.[7] AT&T's monopoly would stand for nearly 70 years.

AT&T was structured as a family of companies comprising regional and long-distance service, among other businesses. While MCI was a long-distance company, it depended on integration with the regional Bell companies for service. In 1974, as a result of Illinois Bell disconnecting local access from MCI, MCI sued AT&T for antitrust. In 1980, a jury awarded MCI nearly $2 billion and within two years, AT&T agreed to divest the regional operating companies.[8] With regional restrictions gone, MCI became a force in long-distance services.

The mid-1990s was a heady time for the telecommunications industry. The growth of the Internet was increasing demand for communications equipment and services. The deregulation of the telecommunications industry opened up a huge market for cut-rate long-distance from different sources, such as phone cards and 900 numbers. Resellers became a large part of MCI's business, but the growth of these contracts required financing; financing MCI was happy to provide.

In 1995, Walt Pavlo was a manager in the carrier finance department of MCI. At the front lines of the growth in the reseller business, the carrier finance department had tripled its collections volume in the three years Pavlo had been with MCI. Pavlo's specialty was high-risk accounts, which meant collecting difficult receivables or finding other ways to get the money. The stress of the job increased as business grew, but when he approached his superiors about the large increase in bad debt, his superiors replied that he needed to find a way to address it. The pressure to meet unrealistic targets generated ever more creative ways to address the problem. Adding to Pavlo's frustration was that, based on site visits, he knew there was cash available to the customers to pay the debt. Unfortunately, the resellers were often very shady operations. Caught between customers who refused to pay and superiors who refused to

(Continued)

acknowledge a problem, Pavlo did not think the $70,000 he earned a year was worth the trouble. He was concerned for his job, worried about legal liability, and began to drink heavily.

After a social meeting at a bar, Pavlo and several others hit on a solution: set up an intermediary company to factor the resellers' receivables. Factoring usually involves buying a company's accounts receivable at a discount. The company—in this case MCI—receives cash immediately and the factoring institution collects the cash from the company's customer. In this case, they set up a factoring company that factored MCI's receivables and the receivables of the reseller. This allowed the factoring company to collect directly from the resellers' customers. The catch was that MCI needed to guarantee any shortfall. Desperate for a solution, Pavlo agreed and committed MCI to the guarantee even though he had no authority to do so.

Once that line was crossed, the next step came more easily. Pavlo and his associates began to strong arm MCI customers into the factoring deal, but the factoring company would not pay MCI; it would send the money to the Caymans and Pavlo used accounting tricks and his position at MCI to cover the unpaid bill at MCI. Once up and running, Pavlo and his associates siphoned off $6 million in under a year. In January 1997, the scheme fell apart; Pavlo quit and was eventually sentenced to 41 months in prison.[9]

Leadership Perspective

What was he thinking? Walt Pavlo's fall from hard worker to felon was sadly typical. He was just your average middle manager trying to do as well as he could in his job. He was clearly ambitious and aggressive, though apparently no more so than most. The beginning of the problems seemed to start at the end of 1995, when, according to Pavlo, "MCI's budget for bad debt was about $15 million a year. 'I sent a memo to senior staff telling them that we had about $180 million of bad debt for 1996 and asking how we were going to address it,' he remembers. 'The response I received was that the bad debt budget for 1996 was going to remain at $15 million and that we would just have to work through whatever issues we had.'"[10] Not only were the expectations unrealistic, it became clear that senior management was perfectly happy to look the other way when it came to questionable accounting practices. The reseller business was a large contributor to profits—though those profits were, of course, illusory—and no one seemed anxious to shoot the goose while it was laying the golden eggs.

Shooting the messenger, on the other hand, was not out of the question. The deeper and deeper Pavlo got into the shady practices of MCI's reseller division, the more he realized that at some point the situation was going to come to light and he was going to be the scapegoat. If he was going to take the fall, why shouldn't he be compensated for his risk? Under normal circumstances, Walt Pavlo probably would not have considered defrauding MCI and its customers, but with his "safety need" of financial security severely threatened, his moral compass became altered enough to do so. "Pavlo notes that, at the time he stepped over the line, he had no remorse, believing he was not alone in his deceptions. He now sees that as the oldest justification in the book, reaching beyond entitlement into confirmation. 'These people are doing it,' he says. 'I looked up to them. They're having to fudge, they're not going to mind if I do too.'"[11] Pavlo's moral compass snapped back once the money started rolling in and he felt his safety need satisfied. He could not sleep and began to drink more and more. Of course, the consequences were severe, including nearly two years in jail and the demise of his marriage.

THERE BUT FOR THE GRACE OF GOD

We need to acknowledge the practical difficulties in assessing individual psychological traits. Clearly there are firms that perform psychological profiles, and many organizations require one as part of the employment process; but there is no reason to believe someone like Walt Pavlo would have raised any red flags. Simply because someone is under stress, either from work or home, does not indicate that fraud is on the horizon. Individuals deal with stress constantly and the vast majority of people work through these tough times. In any organization, the higher one climbs the ladder, the more stress one can expect. How many senior executives do you know that live a stress-free life? Finally, stress has a positive context: It indicates one cares about the outcome of the circumstances. Walt Pavlo wanted to do a good job for his employer and the stress he experienced started with his concern that he could not meet the expectation of his superiors regardless of the reasonableness of those expectations.

So, without hard and fast numbers, what can we glean from this case? This case demonstrates a few important points generally. First, anyone is susceptible to unethical or criminal behavior given the right set of circumstances. Luckily, the vast majority of your employees will not be tested as to their limits, but any member of your organization is vulnerable. Depending on the sphere of moral development they have attained and the level of self-awareness they have, individuals will react differently to the pressures exerted on them.

Next, complex fraud involves multiple players, both active and passive. In this instance, there were three coconspirators and only one of them was an employee—Pavlo—of MCI. There were, however, many passive participants at MCI. Managers and fellow employees of Pavlo's division were actively involved in concealing the problem of bad debt from the company, shareholders, and the public. In this case, however, unethical decisions were commonplace and Pavlo took it to the next level.

High-profile frauds such as Enron and WorldCom involved multiple employees acting in concert. These and the MCI case show where *environmental actors* play a part; that is, multiple individuals making decisions in a particular environment, a concept discussed in more detail in Chapter 6. Complex frauds do more damage, but should be "easier" to detect as it requires the combination of low moral maturity, low self-awareness, and low self-control to be present in multiple parties. In complex conspiracies, a needs deficiency is not required by all parties at the outset. While this will be discussed in Chapter 6 as well, in complex corporate conspiracies involving superiors and subordinates, the needs deficiency can be created by the manager when none existed.

BROKEN WINDOWS

The last lesson is the slippery slope. In the vast majority of cases, corporate malfeasance is a progression from small offenses to large ones. This is the corporate version of the Broken Windows Theory, which holds that once little problems are accepted, the problem will grow. Once the bigger problems become accepted, they will continue to grow, and so on. While the Broken Window Theory has its detractors, the original authors observed that "[u]ntended property becomes fair game for people out for fun or plunder and even for people who ordinarily would not dream of doing such things and who probably consider themselves law-abiding."[12] Adopting it to our analysis, we can observe that people in your organization will consider unethical behavior that goes unpunished as "accepted." Once the line on "acceptable" behavior has been redrawn, what is, in fact, unacceptable behavior becomes in doubt. Given the sketchy practices of Pavlo's division and its acceptance as standard practice, the step to criminal fraud was not as immense as it should have been.

The instant case is illustrative of a particular set of circumstances from which we can draw some generalization, but there are a few more points that warrant discussion. First, it is important to note that it is not only the work environment that puts pressures on employees. Financial or family problems are also a major factor of stress in the workplace. Because the time at work ends up consuming much of our waking hours, regardless of the source of stress, stress will often manifest itself at the office. Further, as pressure mounts to the point where a breaking point is reached, how poor decisions or behavior will manifest itself will be dependent on the opportunity, not on where the stress comes from.

Next, corporate misconduct is not an act of passion, but one of thought. It is not impulsive, but rather the result of a personal profile and circumstances.[13] While moral maturity and self-awareness are difficult to observe, self-control is observable within the workplace environment and also in nonwork-related activities. Research suggests that serious misconduct shares similar psychological traits as certain noncriminal behaviors, such as gambling, or a person's frequent involvement in auto or work accidents. But correlation is not causation and we should emphasize that it is not that they will be involved in misconduct, only that the tendency to lack self-control in one area of a person's life can carry over into other areas, in particular in times of stress.

RENDING MORAL FABRIC

In this chapter, we have tried to develop a framework for the individual decision making at the heart of unethical behavior. Many people familiar with corporate malfeasance will recognize the Fraud Triangle as a simple way to construct the environment of fraudulent activity. The three phases of the Fraud Triangle are composed of components that relate to individual decision making and environmental factors. We have melded a number of elements into an overarching framework to explain why individuals behave badly. At the heart of this framework are three elements that are intertwined to create a profile of how susceptible an individual is to misconduct. The first part is the moral maturity of an individual, which forms the general context of the decision-making process. Individuals operate in three spheres of moral maturity that are based on Kohlberg's Levels of Moral Development. What sphere one resides in is dependent on the primary way one approaches ethical decision making. The lowest level is the self sphere, which focuses only on the individual's own judgment as to what constitutes moral or ethical behavior irrespective of what others think. The most common level is the social sphere, where one bases one's action not only on the individual's own frame of reference, but on what constitutes proper behavior among family, friends, and society. The vast majority of individuals operate in the social sphere. Finally, the highest level is the societal sphere, where the individual views actions in a more abstract way and looks at not only what is expected, but what is right. This last group is the least likely to commit fraud and exhibits qualities that are very beneficial to the organization.

Thus the individual has an innate and constant moral framework to make decisions. This framework is tested by needs deficiencies based on Maslow's Hierarchy of Needs. In particular, safety needs, such as financial security, that are lacking or perceived to be lacking in an employee's life will cause stress and pressure on the person's moral framework and may lead to misconduct under certain circumstances. While the vast majority of employees will never commit corporate malfeasance, no one is immune from these pressures and every individual is susceptible given an extreme needs deficiency.

Finally, the link between the psychological framework of the three spheres and the pressures of the needs deficiency is the nexus between self-awareness and self-control. Self-awareness is the individual recognition of his or her moral framework and what constitutes right and wrong. Self-control is the behavior manifestation of this self-awareness and acts as a brake on bad behavior. The less self-aware an individual is, the less self-control that individual will demonstrate. Further, lack of self-control reveals itself in ways that are not considered illicit and may indicate a greater propensity to commit misconduct.

Of course, the act of decision making does not occur in a vacuum. The external environment has a tremendous influence on a person's action. This is the topic of Chapter 6.

■ NOTES

1. Low-level law breaking is far more prevalent than most realize or admit. Who actually drives the speed limit?
2. There have been large cities throughout history, but populations seemed to have changed drastically. In 7,000 BCE, the largest city in the world was Jericho, with between 1,000 and 2,000 people. The first city over 100,000 was thought to be Ur in modern Iraq. In 200 BCE, the city of Alexandria was

estimated to contain 600,000 people and 100 years later, Alexandria's population was estimated to be 1 million. In contrast, the city of Paris in the late
fourteenth century had an estimated population of 275,000. (Source:
George Modelski, *World Cities: −3000 to 2000* (Washington, DC: Faros,
2003)).

3. For a discussion on Kohlberg's stages, see W. C. Crain., *Theories of Development* (Englewood Cliffs, NJ: Prentice-Hall, 1985), pp. 118–136.

4. A. H. Maslow, "A Theory of Human Motivation," *Psychological Review* 50
   (1943): 370–396.

5. *Needs* should not be interpreted broadly. For example, divorce might lead to
   a needs deficiency on a safety (financial) and social level, but the divorce in
   and of itself does not drive aberrant behavior.

6. This case study, as with every case study, derives it content from a variety of
   sources, primarily contemporary newspaper and periodical accounts. For a
   complete and powerful account of Mr. Pavlos's story, see Walter Pavlo and
   Neil Weinberg, *Stolen without a Gun: Confessions from inside History's Biggest
   Accounting Fraud—The Collapse of MCI Worldcom* (Tampa, FL: Etika, 2007).

7. For an overview, see Adam Thierer, "Unnatural Monopoly: Critical
   Moments in the Development of the Bell System Monopoly," *Cato Journal*
   14, no. 2 (1994): 267–285.

8. Ironically, the new AT&T is a result of the merger of several of the operating companies, including Southwestern Bell, Pacific Telesis, Bell South, and
   Ameritech.

9. Neil Weinberg, "Ring of Thieves," *Forbes*, June 10, 2002. Available from
   http://members.forbes.com/forbes/2002/0610/064.html (accessed
   15 January 2009).

10. Mike Jacka, "An Environment for Fraud," *Internal Auditor*, April 2004.
    Available from http://findarticles.com/p/articles/mi_m4153/is_2_61/
    ai_n6152655 (accessed 15 January 2009).

11. *Ibid.*

12. George L. Kelling and James Q. Wilson, "Broken Windows," *Atlantic
    Monthly,* March 1982. Available from http://www.theatlantic.com/doc/
    198203/broken-windows (accessed 15 January 2009).

13. There are, of course, criminal acts in the workplace that are crimes of
    passion, but the focus is misbehavior related to the workplace, rather than
    general criminal activity.

CHAPTER 6

Work Environment and Group Dynamics

Men are disturbed not by things, but by the view which they take of them.

—EPICTETUS

SOCIAL ANIMALS

Humans are social creatures. From ancient times, when we hunted in packs, to enjoying a pint at the local watering hole, social acceptance is a powerful force in our lives. We all want to be liked and respected by those we like and respect. As discussed in Chapter 5, most individuals operate on the social sphere, where their standards of behavior are influenced not only by their own internal moral compass, but by the accepted behaviors of their friends, associates, and society. Further, actions by individuals that lie outside the standards of behavior, in particular when those actions do not meet the standards of behaviors, are frowned upon and there is a large amount of corrective pressure to conform to the norms.

In Chapter 5, we took a look at what psychological and behavioral factors are at play when an individual faces a moral decision. What goes through someone's mind is an interesting and necessary part of analyzing decision making and, as we will discuss in Chapter 9, how to "help" individuals in making the right decision. But in addition to our own internal moral compass and decision-making process, people are heavily influenced by external factors. In any organizational setting, the external influences can be viewed in three ways. First is the overall business atmosphere. This encompasses all the high-level perceptions of the work environment, including reputation, mission, vision, values, and culture. Most important, these are the impressions or information that an employee derives *indirectly* or through third parties. This category is not what an individual observes day to day but what they hear or read from third parties, whether the third party is a company executive, newsletter, or rumor mill.

The second group dynamic is the small group. These are the people whom the individual interacts with regularly within the organization. These people, in turn, interact with others who are part of a specific section, such as the finance department; but this category will also include those outside the immediate physical environment and extends to contacts throughout the organization. Certain groups, such as human resources, have extensive contacts outside their department, while others will be more local. This category also includes coworkers who socialize together. The critical distinguishing feature is the direct contact between employees. Thus, the employee no longer has to interpret what someone else says the facts are or what they read, but can assess the input directly through their own experiences.

Finally, the last group is the chain of command, which includes the employees' immediate superior and those in charge above the employee's boss. This is a special group of influencers because of the disproportion amount of power they wield over the employee. Further, the boss is a proxy for all of management, for better or worse. This combination of power and authority makes the chain of command perhaps *the* critical component in the environmental influences on an employee. We will look at each of these influences in turn and examine how much impact the environment has on an employee's behavior and how deep the impact is. As one might imagine, each category influences an employee's decision making more than the prior category, but each category represents a greater challenge for a company to influence the message, control disinformation, or counter a rumor.

Now, it is taken for granted that the idea that group conventions influence individual behavior is uncontroversial, but we should take a moment to examine this a bit more. Certainly, in the standard Fraud Triangle model, the environmental influences are apparent in the elements of opportunity—that is, the circumstances under which malfeasance may occur, and pressure, which may come from individual circumstances or environmental circumstances. An example is found in the Walt Pavlo Case Study from Chapter 5, where it is clear that the pressure of meeting corporate goals was a contributing factor in the decision to commit fraud. The why and how are important for an organization to understand, so that it may discourage unethical behavior and encourage ethical behavior.

RELATIVE ETHICS

To quote the sociologist Emile Durkheim, "Before embarking on this particular question, it is important to establish the general principle that the domain of the genuinely moral life only begins where the collective life begins—or, in other words, that we are moral beings to the extent that we are social beings."[1] That morality depends on society should be clear: Imagine you are alone on a desert island. Whether any action you take is "moral" or "immoral" is largely irrelevant. In this case, *you* make the rules, and while you may draw on your experiences prior to being stranded on the island, the fact is conditions dictate what you consider right or wrong. On a desert island, moral is what you say it should be because there is no one else to judge otherwise.[2] As soon as someone else enters the picture, the situation changes. Assuming the other person is a peer—that is, someone who can reasonably contribute to the survival effort—the two survivors will find that cooperating will lead to a greater benefit to both than trying to go it alone. But cooperating means establishing rules and the presence of agreed upon rules is a prerequisite for establishing what constitutes acceptable or ethical behavior. In addition, what these two desert islanders consider ethical behavior may be different than what was considered ethical behavior in polite society, in particular when survival is at stake.[3]

So, while there is a common foundation to human morality, what constitutes the full extent of ethical behavior is not set in stone. There are universal rules that most humans believe, but much of what constitutes acceptable behavior for a certain part of human interaction depends on the circumstances of the group in question. The United States has a certain ethical culture that is different than, though it shares many common elements with, Australia or Japan. Within the United States, different groups, whether we are speaking of a corporation, governmental entity, civic group, or something else, will have an ethical culture slightly different than the country or other groups. The ethical culture and standards of behavior are dependent on many things, though it is primarily driven by the purpose of the organizations and the means the organization uses to achieve its purpose. Health care organizations have different standards of treating customer information than a retailer because of the nature of the business and the expectations of the customer. An attorney working for a law firm has different ethical standards than a government attorney. This is not to imply that one set of standards is higher than another, just that they are different. A lawyer in private practice is entrusted to zealously defend his or her client. A government lawyer, however, is expected to see that justice is served, even if that means not "winning" the case. Each standard is suited for that particular role, but conforming to the standard of a government lawyer as an attorney in private practice may lead to unacceptable or unethical behavior. The goal of an organization, posing the issue in the affirmative, is to have the individual conform to, and not deviate from, expected standards of behavior. Thus, by speaking of the influence of organizational environment, small groups and managers, what we mean is whether your organization, its discreet groups, and its managers are able to influence your employees' behavior so that it is in line with the expectations and standards of the organization.

SOCIAL CONTROL THEORY

Whether any individual employee conforms to standards of ethical behavior depends on what criminologists refer to as *social control*.[4] Despite the ominous sounding name, Social Control Theory is less about overt coercion than about social bonding with groups that reflect mutually acceptable values. The group morality must match the morality of the individual to reduce the chance of behaviors that do not conform to expected norms. Any mismatch can cause tension and the greater the discrepancy, the greater the tension. We assume, for the moment, that the standards for behavior are ethical. Now we can look at the four elements that need to be present for an individual to conform to the group behavior. When one or more of these elements are lacking or weakened, the risk of unethical or criminal behavior increases. Further, these elements need to be present in each of the three categories we will be discussing to ensure, to the maximum extent possible, that ethical standards will be met.

One final point is that the social bonding elements we discuss are a double-edged sword and leaders must be conscious of both edges. While we are addressing the question of "Why do good people do bad things?" it is worthwhile to explore the opposite question: "Why don't employees break the rules all the time?" With the question reframed, we might actually find that employees break the rules often, mostly in small ways and sometime in beneficial ways, but rule breaking may be much more common than we would want to admit. For the sake of discussion, we are focusing on what weakens the bond of an employee to a group. Implicit is the idea that the group culture is a positive one and one that advances the interests of the stakeholders of an organization. In addition, we are examining negative factors that will loosen the bonds of an employee to this positive environment. The other possibility is that the group, most likely a department, division, or office within the organization, has a counterproductive culture that the individual bonds with. In this case, the corrective influence is not positive: Groups interested in behaving badly will pressure all members to conform to bad behavior. This will also have a detrimental effect on the organization as a whole and must be avoided. We can use the elements described herein to address both sides of the sword.

CASE STUDY   THE STANFORD PRISON EXPERIMENT

In 1971, for college students, payment of $15 a day was a very attractive offer.[5] After a battery of tests, 24 students were picked to participate for a period of about two weeks in an experiment sponsored by the Department of Psychology at Stanford University. The experiment was run by Dr. Philip Zimbardo, a newly tenured professor at Stanford. The basic experiment was simple, the group was divided up into two subgroups, one designated "guards" and one designated "prisoners." Seventeen rules were read to the prisoners designed to instill a sense of obedience and humiliation. The prisoners were "arrested" by the Palo Alto police and booked at the station before being led to the "prison" and strip searched. The prisoners were no longer referred to by name, but referred to by number, further dehumanizing them. The guards were told to keep order, but not to use violence or force.

After an uneventful first day, the experiment started to deteriorate on the second day. The prisoners "rebelled," barricading themselves in cells and ripping off their identifying numbers. The guards were not told how to react, but among themselves decided to use a fire extinguisher to gain entrance, quell the rebellion, and punish the prisoners. Subsequently, the guards became vastly more aggressive toward the prisoners, including psychological intimidation and physical distress. After a rumor of a prison break, the guards increased the intimidation and even the researchers fell into the role, getting upset when questioned on their methods. Professor Zimbardo went so far as to invite a priest to participate by interviewing the prisoners and telling them they would not leave without the help of a lawyer, which served the purpose of further reinforcing the idea that the experiment was real.

By the fifth day, it became clear that the experiment had grown out of control. At night, when the guards thought the researchers were not watching, the abuse escalated dramatically, greatly concerning Dr. Zimbardo and the researchers. The prisoners became pathological and the guards sadistic. It took the outrage of one person, Christina Maslach, to finally call an end to the experiment. Maslach was the only one of about 50 outsiders who observed the experiment to call into question what was being done.

The Stanford Prison Experiment is one of the most famous psychological experiments of all time, made even more powerful by the admission of the researchers that they, too, fell into an abnormal behavioral pattern to adhere to the "role" they were playing. The experiment had a powerful impact on those who participated, including Dr. Zimbardo, who acted as a witness for the defense of Staff Sergeant Ivan Frederick for his role in the Abu Ghraib prison trial. Looking back almost 40 years, what stands out is how quickly "normal" people turned bad. While the Stanford Prison Experiment involved extraordinary circumstances outside the day-to-day scope of most people's lives, it opens a window into the role of social and group pressure as an influence on behavior. These are influences all of us feel from time to time. It is the pressure of expectations of those whose opinions we care about: our family, our friends, our coworkers, and our bosses. Expectations are not necessarily as bad as the ones at the Stanford Prison, but once established, they are very difficult to change or to rebel.

ELEMENTS OF SOCIAL BONDING

With the Stanford Prison Experiment Case Study as our example, we can return to the four elements of social bonding. The first element is belief in the ethical framework and common value system of the group. Does the employee believe in the stated and unstated values of the organization? Every organization has values and culture. The values are often very well articulated and communicated throughout the organization and to the public. The "About IBM" Web page states first and foremost the "IBMers" company values:

- Dedication to every client's success.
- Innovation that matters—for our company and for the world.
- Trust and personal responsibility in all relationships.[6]

Dedication, innovation, trust, and personal responsibility may be considered IBM's core values, but are these values embraced by the subgroups—the executive suite, finance, legal, sales—and the employees? The degree in which your departments' and employees' core values do not conform to the core values of the organization presents a risk to the organization. Losing faith in the organization, the team, or the manager creates a situation of risk for the organization.

In the Stanford Prison Experiment, the deviation from the norms of the world outside the experiment and the experiment itself became clear early on. One can feel confident in saying that the core values of Stanford University or the psychology department did not include the behaviors exhibited by the participants in the experiment. Further, the descent into deviant behavior affected everyone from the "prisoners" to Professor Zimbardo and his staff. It was only an outsider who recognized the extent of the problem. Yet, given the circumstances, is it correct to say that the prison experiment group abandoned the core values? Or is it more accurate to say that the core values of the small group were subsumed by a greater priority? The lesson here is particularly appropriate as the pressure for improved performance of all organizations increase: The goals of the experiment became the core value of the group to the exclusion of all others.

The next element is attachment. Your employees will develop attachments to and within the organization. In this case, attachment means a bond or tie with individuals or groups. The bonds may be few or many, but some level of bonds will be present. Attachment comes into play because when an employee attaches to your organization and the groups within the organization, that employee begins to relate to the group and care about the perceptions of the group. As attachments grow, the group's opinion of the individual becomes more important and begins to shape behavior. The individual starts to view actions and performance through the lens of what is acceptable or unacceptable to the group. As attachments to the group weaken—as when other members of the group leave or friction develops between members—the desire for an individual's action to be accepted by the group also weaken and behavior that deviates from expectations becomes more of a risk.

As we saw in the Stanford Prison Experiment Case Study, conforming behavior was quickly adopted by the various groups. Also, conforming behavior was reinforced by the group to make sure that all members of the group complied: The most rebellious anyone became was acceptance instead of participation in the activities, but tacit acceptance has the effect of encouraging bad behavior further. Additionally, each group, as they played their part, buttressed the actions of the other groups. The acquiescence of the "prisoners," for example, encouraged the "guards" to continue their behavior and did not send the appropriate signals to Professor Zimbardo and his team that this was unacceptable behavior. The behavior became self-perpetuating until an external actor interceded. Andrew Jackson once said, "One man with courage makes a majority." In this case, it took one woman with courage to intervene and put an end to the behavior.

The element of attachment also brings up a corresponding issue: namely, that an individual will develop social bonds to groups outside the organization that also influence behavior. Further, in a world of competing attachments, seeking acceptance of the group most important to the individual, whether work, family, church, or other, becomes the driving factor. To the extent that each group the individual is attached to espouses the same values, the chances of behavior deviating from the groups' expectation become very low. This becomes an important element in helping an organization fight unethical behavior, which we examine in greater detail in Chapter 10.

Once attachments form, the element of commitment measures how deep those attachments are. Commitment amounts to the resources an individual has invested in the group. The types of resources committed are important to this discussion. While resources are often described in terms of time and effort, the most underappreciated component is publicity. Publicity has a multiplier effect on time and effort. The more an individual's time and effort is publicly tied to a group, the less likely the individual will engage in behavior detrimental to the group. Publicity turns the resources of time and effort into associations that further deepen commitment to the group.

The final element of social bonding is involvement. Involvement is the number of different activities an individual participates in within the group. The more activities an employee gets involved in, the greater the bond to the group. Furthermore, time spent participating in multiple activities reduces the time available for nefarious pursuits and gives the individual a broader perspective of the group and the impact the individual and the group have in the larger organization. The more an individual or group "silos" or "stovepipes," the less of a bond they will have with the organization.

The four elements of social bonding provide a framework to discuss the way groups influence individual behavior. The greater the bond between the individual and the group, the less risk there is for behavior outside of the norms and expectations of the group. The bonds to the organization and its component groups weaken when the individual does not believe in the values and mission espoused by the organization or the functional group. Bonds will also weaken based on a lack of attachment to the groups. Attachments are based on ties with elements of the group, such as other members.

A lack of commitment puts the group at risk for unethical behavior. Commitment involves the devotion of time and effort to the group, though time and effort without public association is often not enough. Finally, the less involved a person is with the organization or group, the less of a bond is formed. An individual who is siloed in their job will be at greater risk for unethical behavior than a person involved in a broad spectrum of group activities.

At the beginning of this chapter, three external influences on an individual were discussed. The final influence is the chain of command that the employee reports to, in particular, the employee's immediate supervisor. It cannot be emphasized enough the disproportionate influence a boss has on his or her subordinate, but to drive home the point, we look at another groundbreaking experiment in psychology.

CASE STUDY   THE MILGRAM EXPERIMENT

Lest one's regional prejudices lead one to believe that the Stanford Prison Experiment was a result of crazy hippies out in California, we can also turn back the clock to July 1961 and travel across the country to New Haven, Connecticut, and the campus of Yale University. Presaging the experiment at Stanford, an ad in the local newspaper offered $4.50 for one hour's work to take part in a psychology experiment investigating memory and learning. Once the participant arrived, the participant answering the ad was assigned to be the "teacher" and another participant, who was actually a hired actor, was to be the "student." The roles were determined by drawing lots, but the drawing was rigged so the outcome was predetermined, even though the teacher/participant did not realize that at the time. The assignment was supervised by an experimenter who immediately and sternly assumed the role of an authority figure.

(Continued)

The student was then taken to an adjoining room where he was strapped in a chair to prevent movement and an electrical device was attached to his arm. The teacher was situated in a room with an electrical generator under the watchful eye of the experimenter. The teacher was instructed to read a list of word pairs and ask the learner to recite the second word after the teacher said the first word and offered several optional second words. If the learner recited the correct word pair, the teacher would recite the next word pair. If the learner was incorrect, the teacher would administer a shock. In reality, there was no shock administered, but a prerecorded cry based on the voltage level was broadcast for the teacher to hear. Starting out at 15 volts, the punishment reached a maximum "punishment" of 450 volts.[7] At later stages, the learner would pound on the wall and complain about a "bad heart." Later still, the learner would fall silent.

The final piece of the puzzle was the experimenter who would press the teacher if they became reluctant to administer the shock. The experimenter would urge the teacher to continue with four different, though increasingly harsh, directives. If the teacher still desired to stop after that, the experiment stopped. The experiment would finally cease after the maximum voltage was administered three consecutive times.

Of course, this experiment had nothing to do with teaching and memory, but was an experiment of the effect of authority figures on behavior. In a poll of psychology students prior to the experiment, respondents expected only a very few would administer the maximum dose of electricity. In reality, 65 percent of "teachers" completed the experiment by administering the final shock. Only one participant refused to continue before 300 volts. The Milgram Experiment remains one of the most famous psychology experiments in history and reminds us of the power authority figures have in influencing behaviors.

POWER, AUTHORITY, AND PROXIMITY

Sixty-five percent administered the maximum voltage for $4.50 per hour of income. This amount translates into approximately $32 per hour or $66,000 annually today. There were no threats of being fired, no physical threats. There was just a verbal push with a stern demeanor, the harshest of which was "You have no other choice, you *must* go on." The lesson is clear: The face of authority has a disproportionate influence on behavior. While that may come as no surprise, what should be surprising is the degree.

In the Stanford Prison Experiment, the "prisoners" tolerated a substantial amount of abuse from "guards" who were just acting the part, and the prisoners turned on each other if it gave them an advantage with the guards. The guards, for their part, readily adapted to the role of the authority figure and abused this power when they were given the opportunity. Most interesting, the professors who ran the experiment became too focused on what the outcome would be and, consequently, lost the broader perspective of what means they were taking to justify their ends. Professor Zimbardo even harshly reacted to those who would question his methods . . . and those individuals backed down.[8]

The Milgram Experiment offers a more pointed example. Note how unexpected the actual results were to psychology students; their prediction of level of abuse was well below actual observed abuse. Nor were Milgram's statistics a fluke. In the time since the first experiment, others who have replicated the experiment have produced similar results:[9] Fully two-thirds of the participant "teachers" will continue to produce shocks until the experiment is stopped and administer them over the protests of the "learner." Milgram's experiments were designed to measure the effect of an authority figure on the behavior of an individual with startling results, but these results inform us in creating an ethical environment. While the influence of authority figures can have a detrimental impact on the behaviors of your employees, they can also be used for the betterment of the company.

POSITIVE PEER PRESSURE

In Chapter 5, we discussed the psychological propensities of the individual to unethical behavior. In this chapter, we looked at the influence of groups on individual behavior and, in particular, what circumstances are necessary for nonconforming behavior to occur. There are three basic groups that the individual will associate within your organization and certain elements of social control that enable the group to exert influence—negative or positive—on the individual. The first is the organization itself. The organization establishes the overall core value system and, hopefully, lives this system in their actions. The organization is represented to the individual indirectly through general communications—reputation and rumor—and other ways not directly impacting the individual but influencing the individual's overall understanding and perception of the organization. Direct contact is made by a smaller group or groups, usually an office, a department, or other functional group, other employees with whom the individual interacts with as part of their job, and, possibly, social groups. Where the overall organization is an influencing factor, the small group exerts a great deal of peer pressure to conform to the standards established by that group.

The chances that an individual will conform to the behavior of the group are determined by four elements of social control. The first is belief in the values and mission of the group. Belief in the overall values allows the individual to get beyond immediate issues that may present the individual with difficult choices, choices that are made easier by the belief in an overall guiding principle. The second element is attachment—that is, the bond developed with the individuals within the group. The more attachments to the group, the more influence the group's approval or expectations will exert on individual behavior.

Commitment represents the depth of the attachments to the group and manifests itself through the resources an individual commits to the success of the group. The types of resources include measurable items such as time and effort, but to the extent that an individual's commitment is made public and therefore develops an association between the individual and the group, the committed resources can be leveraged to the benefit of the group and individual. Finally, the last element is involvement with various activities within the group. Involvement gives the individual a broader perspective and appreciation of the group's values and mission and, in an ethical organization, promotes positive behaviors.

The last special case is the influence of managers and other authority figures on the individual's behavior. The combination of power and proximity creates a unique situation of influence on an individual. The Milgram Experiment and its progeny over the years indicate a very high degree of conformity to the wishes of an authority figure by individuals even though the individuals understand that their actions may be detrimental. "I was just doing my job" may seem like an adequate reason for acting against principle, but it is an unacceptable excuse in a high-functioning organization.

■ NOTES

1. Emile Durkheim, *Moral Education*, Everett K. Wilson and Herman Schnurer, trs. (New York: Free Press of Glencoe, 1961), 64.
2. We are speaking of social morality, of course, not religious morality, which is subject to the judgment of a higher power.
3. On October 13, 1972, Uruguayan Air Force Flight 571 crashed in the Andes Mountains. The survivors quickly ran out of food and made the agonizing decision to eat the deceased passengers to survive. Sixteen survivors managed to stay alive for 72 days until rescuers found them. Their story was the basis for the book *Alive: The Story of the Andes Survivors* by Piers Paul Read. Was this an ethical decision?
4. While Social Control Theory evolved from the works of many, the basis for much of the theoretical discussion here is the work of Travis Hirschi and, in particular, his book *Causes of Delinquency* (Berkeley, CA: University of California Press, 1969).
5. This summary was composed based on the Stanford Prison Experiment Web site at www.prisonexp.org.
6. International Business Machines Corp., "About IBM," *IBM.com*. Available from http://www.ibm.com/ibm/us/en/ (accessed 19 January 2009).

7. As a point of reference, touching a live wire in your house will typically give you a quick 110 volt shock.

8. Professor Zimbardo did heed the advice of Ms. Maslach, but both enjoyed a particularly close relationship and would eventually marry. One questions whether Dr. Zimbardo would have reacted the same if the relationship had been more distant.

9. The 2006 experiment is explained at the personal Web page of Dr. Jerry Burger of the University of Santa Clara, http://www.scu.edu/cas/psychology/faculty/burger.cfm.

CHAPTER 7

Leadership

If you lead on the people with correctness, who will dare not to be correct?

—CONFUCIUS

TONE AT THE TOP

Leadership.

There is no more important component to your organization than its leadership. The senior leaders—such as the board, CEO, president, and executive management—form the foundation of everything that happens in an organization. While in the past few years more attention has been paid to the role of middle management and employees, the issue of senior leadership is so core to the development of an ethical and effective organization that without it, over the long term, everything else falls apart.

In speaking of leadership, we should not confuse this concept with management. When we speak of management, we are talking about things and processes. Good management increases the efficiency of an organization and allows the employees of an organization—senior leaders and others—to do what it is the organization does. But management is about structure and does not necessarily have to provide leadership to achieve its ends. A successful organization will have a number of very good managers, but they are not necessarily leaders.

Leadership is about people. Leadership is about developing and realizing the potential of the employees of your organization. It is about the human element and driving efficiency of time and commitment to objectives. The human side is much more fragile than processes. A well-documented process may last, but your employee base will change year to year and without the dedication to create the right environment consistently, your people become a wasted asset.

The half-life of a typical leadership effort to advance your organization is between 6 and 12 months.

Six to 12 months.

After that, the residual effect of your leaders' effort to drive performance improvements will have degraded 50 percent unless it is reinforced.

With this in mind, we can look at what makes an effective leader. As discussed in Chapter 6, individuals have three spheres of moral engagement, and their ethical framework results from where they "reside" on this spectrum. When hiring leaders, care must be taken to find individuals who exhibit the characteristics of all three spheres. Hiring an organizational leader who "resides" at a lower level will limit the level at which the organization as a whole will operate. A leader operating at the self sphere cannot drive an organization beyond that sphere. It is the same with those potential leaders operating at the social sphere trying to get the organization to a higher level of performance. It will not happen.

We should acknowledge upfront that different circumstances require leaders of different skills. That does not change the limitations put on the organization by the leadership. For example, you may need a top executive with a special skill set in raising capital, building process controls, or developing new markets because that is an area that requires critical attention in the short term. You should be cognizant of the fact that having such a leader solves a management problem, not a leadership problem. Those skills may be what are nec-essary, but it does not make that person the right leader for the orga-nization. Of course, this is not to say that great managers cannot be great leaders or vice versa; it is more of a reminder that the two do not necessarily go hand in hand.

It should also be noted that an executive who operates in only the social sphere will act differently than an executive operating in the societal spheres. Put another way, the leader operating at the societal sphere manifests the self sphere characteristics differently than a per-son who is just operating at the self sphere. The same holds true for the social sphere.

AUTHENTICITY

When we think about qualities in leaders, we usually focus on virtues such as honesty, integrity, and a strong work ethic. We look for a leader with character. General Norman Schwarzkopf famously said, "Leadership is a combination of strategy and character. If you must be without one, be without the strategy." As said in a previous chap-ter, the vast majority of people are (or at least seem to be) honest, possess integrity, and work hard. Further, the executive selection pro-cess usually focuses on the candidate selling themselves or expressing their positive attributes, while the interviewer searches for the lack of certain qualities. Trying to find the absence of a quality is far more difficult than looking for the presence of a quality. Further, an authentic leader must not only lead in good times, but also during times of stress on the company and its personnel. It is during these "black swan"[1] events that the true mettle of your leadership emerges. But while it is difficult to ascertain how a leader will react in the face of large challenges or opportunities, we can look at a potential leader through the prism of behaviors of the different moral spheres to extrapolate the general indicators that the person you want to hire is the leader you need.

First, authentic leaders are people who are self-aware. As distinct from the problem of egoism posed by individuals who are mired at the self sphere, leaders show an understanding of and comfort in their strengths and limitations. There is balance between self-confidence and humility that gives you and others confidence that the leader understands the importance of each employee's contribution. An authentic leader understands his or her importance to the team, but knows that without the team, goals will not be accomplished. A leader who is self-aware trusts himself or herself to make the right decision.

Authentic leaders are effective at communicating and connecting with people. Both are equally important. Effective communication is critical as a leader. Further, the communication must be clear, concise, and consistent. Goals and objectives need to be defined and values promoted. If you were to ask your organization, "What will we be doing in five years?" the answers should be the same from top to bottom. Unless the organization is clear on its mission, vision, values, and goals, it cannot live up to them or achieve them.

But successfully communicating ideas, goals, and the mission of the company is only one half of the challenge. A leader must connect with stakeholders and the stakeholders must connect with the leader. The best leaders can have a cordial meeting with the Board or a fellow CEO in the morning and be out on the shop floor in the afternoon talking to a machinist. An authentic leader is both respected and admired, *but* also someone who respects and admires others and can show that respect and admiration naturally. This person is easy to like, but he or she also finds it easy to like others. Trust between people is formed from mutual appreciation and understanding.

Finally, an authentic leader understands his or her impact in the community and the market. An authentic leader is deeply concerned about personal, professional, and corporate reputation. They understand that actions impact those we know and those we do not know. By positively impacting those people beyond the stakeholders[2] of the organization, a leader prepares the battlespace for the future. By building goodwill with the world beyond what we see and interact with daily, a leader creates a reserve of trust that is there to draw upon when needed.

It will inevitably be needed.

A final comment: When we say that someone is operating at the societal sphere, keep in mind that it means that the person has shown an understanding of the balance in all three spheres. Balance in the spheres means being functional in each different sphere. Too much "emphasis" in one sphere over the other results in behavior that values that sphere over others. One imagines that the activists who are so focused on the good of the world that they ignore companions, family, and personal hygiene may find themselves without a healthy balance in life. As a corporate leader, such a person would be a disaster. Balance is necessary so that the authentic leader approaches tasks and goals with each sphere in mind and each carrying importance.

CASE STUDY   VÁCLAV HAVEL[3]

FACTS

Václav Havel was born into a wealthy and influential Czech family in 1936. At the end of World War II with the ascent of the Communist regime in Prague, his family lost their wealth and prominence, which were taken away by the Communists as a result of their bourgeois background. Also as a consequence of his family's prior stature, after completing his primary education, young Havel was denied entry into the university. By background and inclination, he became interested in theater and literary pursuits and studied drama in the early 1960s. Havel's natural wit found an outlet: His first play, a satire of the bureaucracy, was a hit in Czechoslovakia and abroad and made a name for him in literary circles. But his interest in politics was ever present. In addition to writing, Havel also led literary and political groups, such as the Club of Independent Writers, was a member of the political group the Club of Engaged Non-Partisans, and worked at the monthly *Tvar,* a non-Marxist publication.

(Continued)

In 1965, about the time Havel joined *Tvar,* Czechoslovakia suffered economically from the failure of central plan-
ning. More progressive elements in the government
engaged managers to help liberalize the economic model.
By 1967, as economic reforms were made, pressure began
to build for even further political reforms to the point where
Stalinist elements in government asked the Soviet Union
to intervene. Soviet president Leonid Brezhnev declined to
do so, which served to encourage the reformists. In 1967,
reformist Alexander Dubçek became First Secretary of
the Communist Party and introduced political freedoms in
the spring of 1968. Learning from the bloody experience
of the 1956 Hungarian Revolution,[4] the Czechoslovakian
leaders were careful to couch the reforms in language meant
to placate the Soviets and signed the Bratislava Declaration
of fidelity to Marxist-Leninist principles.

Hard-line Communists were not fooled or placated. In late
August, forces of the Warsaw Pact—the Soviet-led counter-
part of NATO—invaded Czechoslovakia. President Dubçek
urged the people not to resist. During the invasion, Václav
Havel provided commentary on Radio Free Czechoslovakia.
After the "Prague Spring," Havel's plays were banned and,
as a result of his role in the reformist movement, he could
only get a job as a brewery laborer. Deeply affected by the
failure of the Prague Spring, Havel continued to press for
freedom and reform and was arrested by the government on
several occasions for speaking out on issues. In 1977, a
Czechoslovakian rock band, The Plastic People of the Uni-
verse,[5] was arrested, tried, and sentenced to jail for disturb-
ing the peace. This incident was the spark that led Havel and
others to write the human rights document "Charter 77."
The document was an indictment of Communist government
and its abuses of the citizenry. In reaction, Havel and his
founding cohorts were tried and sentenced to jail. Havel was
in and out of prison for the next dozen years.

In 1989, the country experienced a second attempt at another Prague Spring with the Velvet Revolution, named after
the velvet ropes in the theaters where the opposition met.[6]

Following the collapse of Communism in Poland, Hungary, and East Germany, the suppression of student protests in Prague led to large, nonviolent demonstrations. Within 10 days, the Communist Party in Czechoslovakia relinquished power. Because of his prominent role in reformist politics, Havel seemed to be a natural choice to lead the nation, but mindful of history and the contributions of others he insisted Alexander Dubçek be elected speaker of Parliament by the federal assembly. This occurred the day prior to Václav Havel being appointed interim president. In June 1990, he was elected by popular vote and was elected president of the Czech Republic in 1993 and 1998.[7] Widely admired, Havel has been the recipient of numerous awards, including the U.S. Presidential Medal of Freedom, the Philadelphia Liberty Medal, and the Ambassador of Conscience Award.

LEADERSHIP PERSPECTIVE

In many ways, Havel was born to be Havel. The son of parents of particular political leaning, he was denied the "normal" path of a Czech Communist youth of his talents. As an intellectually gifted outsider, he could observe a dysfunctional system without being part of it. In summary, he had both the necessities and opportunity to become the president of Czechoslovakia.

Václav Havel exhibits the qualities of an authentic leader. He has acute self-awareness: his manner is "an alliance of intellectual self-confidence and modest disbelief in his own significance."[8] His personal convictions were continually being put to the test. His involvement with the human rights manifesto "Charter 77" brought him international fame as the leader of the opposition in Czechoslovakia, but it also led to his imprisonment for four years of hard labor. His self-confidence flows from his personal values, which he described as decency, reason, responsibility, sincerity, civility, and tolerance. "I think it is worthwhile to speak the truth, to not be afraid, and to stand up for oneself under any

(Continued)

circumstances. Fear weakens people, but it is necessary to face fear with bravery, which, I am convinced, will prevail in the end."[9] If Havel were bitter or had experienced self-pity, he did not let it show.

His trust in himself led to 13 years in office, which saw radical changes in his nation, including its split with Slovakia, its accession into NATO, and start of the negotiations for membership in the European Union, which was completed in 2004. In less than 20 years, Havel moved from a prison to the president's office[10] and the Czech Republic moved from oppression to scoring top marks for political rights and civil liberties from Freedom House.[11]

Havel also connected with people. Many were introduced to him through his plays and writings. But his works of fiction and plays were less impressive than his honesty and common touch: In a January 1990 New Year's address as president elected by the federal assembly and not yet popularly elected, he told the nation, "The worst thing is that we live in a contaminated moral environment. We fell morally ill because we became used to saying something different from what we thought. We learned not to believe in anything, to ignore one another, to care only about ourselves. Concepts such as love, friendship, compassion, humility or forgiveness lost their depth and dimension, and for many of us they represented only psychological peculiarities. . . ."[12] Like many great political leaders, such as Mohandas Gandhi, Nelson Mandela, and Corazon Aquino, Havel was personally comfortable in the halls of office or on the streets of the city because he spoke plainly and truthfully. Consequently, his words had tremendous power and inspired trust in his audience, a trust he maintained throughout the years.

Finally, Havel understood the importance of building something meaningful with the opportunity presented. His goals were outlined in that New Year's Address just three days after his election: "I dream of a republic independent, free, and democratic, of a republic economically prosperous and yet socially just; in short, of a humane republic that serves the individual and that therefore holds the hope that the individual will serve it in turn. Of a republic of well-rounded people, because without such people it is impossible to solve any of our problems—human, economic, ecological, social, or political. In conclusion, I would like to say that I want to be a president who will speak less and work more. To be a president who will not only look out of the windows of his airplane but who, first and foremost, will always be present among his fellow citizens and listen to them well."[13] Havel sought no retribution and looked always to the future. The goodwill and trust he engendered worldwide proved immensely valuable to his cause and his country.

OUTSIDE PERSPECTIVES

Václav Havel was the right person at the right time for his country. He was an agent of change from within. Often, a change is needed in an organization that is best implemented by a fresh perspective. The rewards of an outsider can be tremendous—Lou Gerstner's tenure at IBM comes to mind—but an outsider also has the difficulty of, to paraphrase the title of Gerstner's memoirs, understanding how to make the elephant dance. If you are going to lead the elephant in a tango, you better make damn sure the elephant knows where you are going and how to follow.

| CASE STUDY | THE SMITHSONIAN INSTITUTION[14] |

FACTS

In 2000, the Smithsonian Institution was struggling. Despite operating support from Congress and an outstanding brand, the Smithsonian was having a difficult time meeting its mission. Created from the estate of British Scientist

(Continued)

James Smithson, the Smithsonian Institution was established in 1846 as a charitable trust. Ironically, Smithson
never travelled to the United States and there is no record of him ever corresponding to anyone, but when
his estate was settled, the bequeath amounted to over
$500,000, a substantial sum in the mid-nineteenth cen-
tury. Smithson's only criteria became the Institution's
mission: the increase and diffusion of knowledge. Today,
with 19 museums, several research centers, and the National Zoo, the Smithsonian is an international leader in
science, history, art, and culture. The Smithsonian's pioneering initiatives and innovative education and outreach
programs continue to advance its mission, and its collections, containing more than 137 million items, only 2 percent of which can be on display at any one time, remain
one of the world's largest compilation of diverse objects
and documents.[15]

While Congress funds operations, the Institution must
seek outside resources for other programs. Faced with a
sprawling structure, the need to raise private funds, and
its secretary (effectively its president) retiring in 1999, the
Regents of the Smithsonian sought a replacement with
financial acumen, strong managerial credentials, and the
ability to raise a lot of money. A small team of outsiders
was tasked with looking for the new secretary. One of the
members of this committee, Lawrence Small, emerged as
the candidate of choice. Small seemed to fit the bill. He
was a banker by profession, starting out with Citibank in
1964. He moved to Fannie Mae in 1991 as its president.
He also had a very diverse background. He spoke Spanish, French, and Portuguese, having started out his career
at Citibank overseas. He was an accomplished flamenco
guitar player and owned a large collection of artifacts
from the world's rainforests. The head of the executive
recruitment committee remarked, "It's hard to imagine a
better person to lead the Smithsonian into the next
millennium."[16] The only challenge seemed to be compensation. Lawrence Small made over $4 million at Fannie

Mae, but as Secretary of the Smithsonian Institution, he could expect only about 10 percent of that figure.

What seemed like an ideal situation deteriorated almost immediately. Within 15 months, the Smithsonian's senior staff was in rebellion. The initial reaction from the outside was relatively muted. In an article on the clashes, it was noted that "it is not surprising that his corporate vision and blunt, sometimes combative management style have collided with decades-old traditions at the Smithsonian. The challenges the Smithsonian faces are emblematic of the cultural clash facing museums and research centers around the country. The clash pits a purist notion of intellectual pursuit against the need to operate efficiently, raise money and draw audiences to compete with the Internet and popular tourist attractions like Disney World."[17]

Others were not so understanding. "'He has become what is surely the most reviled and detested administrator in the institution's history,' wrote Stores L. Olson, the National Museum of Natural History's senior ornithologist, in a letter . . . sent to key lawmakers and the Smithsonian's Regents. Mr. Olson wrote that 'Americans in general and free-thinking scientists in particular do not perform their best in a dictatorship,' and predicted that the 'ruination' of the institution was 'virtually assured unless remedial action is taken very soon.'"[18] By September 2001, four of the then 16 museum directors had resigned or retired.

Small made some high-profile, controversial decisions, including closing the National Zoological Conservation and Research Center in Virginia and accepting a "strings attached" $32 million gift from the Reynolds Foundation, which were protested and overturned. He complained that the Institution's credo was too vague and did away with many of the traditional management structures and practices of the Smithsonian. The Institution was accustomed to a very different approach than Small's personal management style.

(Continued)

Stylistic differences aside, Mr. Small's background—so appealing to the executive committee at the start—started to become a problem. Small was very proud of his artifact collection, but his very public discussions and displays of the item caught the attention of the United States Fish and Wildlife Service. Within a year of taking the position, Small's collection was being investigated as to whether it contained feathers or other items taken from endangered species. He would eventually plead guilty to a federal misdemeanor.

In the years that followed, Small's role in the accounting scandals at Fannie Mae have been investigated. A government report stated that he and a handful of other Fannie Mae executives set an improper "tone at the top" and encouraged employees to meet financial targets no matter what. The result was a $10.6 billion accounting fraud and a fine of $400 million assessed against Fannie Mae.

At the Smithsonian, Small's conduct came under further scrutiny. His compensation package swelled to over $800,000 per year and he enjoyed a lavish expense account. When questioned about expenses, he reacted "with arrogance and a sense of entitlement" according to Senate investigators.[19] He also continued to sit on boards, including Chubb Insurance, which did approximately $500,000 worth of business annually with the Institute.[20] In addition, he and his second in command are reputed to have taken 950 days off during their tenure and other senior Smithsonian staff closely associated with Small were found to have violated ethics policies.

Small resigned in March 2007 after seven years at the Institution.

LEADERSHIP PERSPECTIVE

Hindsight is 20/20, but Lawrence Small was mired in the self sphere focusing primarily on his needs and objectives, while ignoring the intrapersonal aspects of the position and failing to understand the greater role the Smithsonian Institution plays in the minds of its employees, political patrons, and the public at large. The Smithsonian Institution is a near perfect example of an organization that will not thrive unless it is led by someone with strong balance in all three spheres. Its history, its iconic stature, and its mission all demand a certain type of leader. Lawrence Small, despite his success at Citibank and his career at Fannie Mae, was not the right fit.

The Board of Regents also received scathing criticism for the lack of governance of Small and his staff. The Board of Regents, to its credit, owned up to failing to supervise, but it is unclear if they understood why a failure occurred. The Board of Regents expected major changes in the way the Smithsonian Institution was run but was unprepared to change the way they operated. It is tempting to dismiss the failure of Lawrence Small's tenure as a culture conflict or as a fiasco of an executive run amok, but it was clear that the Smithsonian did need to change. The regents understood the need for organizational change but failed to appreciate and embrace their role in that change.

LEADERSHIP BONDING

In the earlier discussion of Václav Havel, we noted how much he was a part of Czech culture. His roots and understanding helped him appreciate the situation, connect with people, and understand the greater purpose of his role. Many leaders who would be considered "great" are products of the organization or group. In situations where an outsider is brought in, such as when a "fresh" perspective is needed or change is critical to the future, it is especially critical that the outsider bond with the organization and its members in order to lead them toward the organization's goals. Much like the employee must believe, attach, commit, and be involved, the leader must also. In no way does this imply the new leader should surrender to the culture of the organization, but in order to move in a direction, continuing along the same path or charting a new course, the group must be prepared to follow. Further, as is evidenced by the extent of the problems within the hierarchy of the Smithsonian, too many individuals within the Smithsonian did follow Lawrence Small's lead. Unfortunately, it was not the example the Board of Regents were hoping would be set.

It should also be noted that there was enough evidence early in Small's tenure that this was not the right fit. Arguably, the fact that Small was part of the external committee to find the new secretary should have caused concern, as well as the substantial pay cut that Small would be required to take. While pay cuts are hardly unknown, Small was asked to cut his pay from $4.2 million to $480,000 without any other upside opportunity, a change that should have prompted deeper questions about Small's objectives.[21] In addition, the staff clashes were early, deep, and bitter. There is every indication that the directors were deeply dissatisfied with Small's management style and seemingly very vocal about their feelings. Opinions of the senior staff should not have dictated the actions of the Regents, but a rebellion that is broad and deep should have prompted additional inquiry. It was clear in contemporaneous reports that director and staff morale had become a large problem. The Regents seemed unprepared for the level of problems that arose.

Self-awareness, effective communication, connection, and a higher sense of purpose are the building blocks of authentic leadership and these attributes are the manifestation of the evolution of the ethical development of an individual outlined in Chapter 6. It may not be politically correct to say so, but not everyone has the intellectual and emotional profile to run an organization. To do so effectively requires foundational attributes, the absence of which fundamentally diminishes the chance of success especially in trying times. There are so many internal and external forces that adversely impact your organization. It is imperative that your leadership has the character to overcome these forces.

It might seem perfectly obvious that these traits are beneficial, but why is the human factor so important? Because of trust. The common factor in these attributes is the element of trust. Self-awareness is trust in one's self. Communication and connection builds personal trust between individuals and an appreciation for the organization's impact on the broader community builds trust with stakeholders— both present and future. Looking at the role of leadership at the highest abstraction, the most important job of leadership is building and maintaining trust. In the next chapter, as we will see, trust is the lifeblood of your organization.

NOTES

1. *Black swan* refers to the theory popularized by Nassim Nicholas Taleb, which states that those events that are rare and unpredictable have the biggest impact on our lives.
2. *First-degree stakeholders* are individuals and organizations that are directly affected by the actions of a company, such as shareholders, employees, vendors, and customers.
3. A special thanks to Prema Srivanasan, who researched this case study.
4. The Hungarian Revolution was a true armed revolt meant to oust the remaining Soviet forces from Hungary and resulted in the deaths of 2,500 Hungarians. The Prime Minister of Hungary, Imre Nagy, was arrested by the Soviets after a promise of free passage, secretly tried, and hanged. As bloody and significant as it was, the Hungarian Revolution was not a revolt against Marxism.
5. The unique name of the band comes from the song "Plastic People" on the 1967 album *Absolutely Free* by Frank Zappa and the Mothers of Invention.
6. According to Havel, who did not coin the term, "Velvet Revolution" came from the band Velvet Underground led by singer Lou Reed whom Havel admired and with whom Havel developed a great friendship.
7. In 1992, Czechoslovakia split into the Czech Republic and Slovakia.
8. Alan Franks, "Vaclav Havel: Life after Revolution," *Times* (London), September 16, 2008, p. T2.
9. Ashok Chopra, "His Best Is Still to Come," *Tribune* (Chandigarh, India), October 4, 1998.
10. Havel is a self-proclaimed reluctant politician. In his book, *Summer Meditations* (New York: Knopf, 1992), he wrote, "the more I am forced to be active in politics, the more I enjoy doing theater."
11. Freedom House, "Czech Republic Country Report," in *Freedom in the World 2008* (Washington, DC: Freedom House/Rowman & Littlefield, 2008).

12. Václav Havel, *New Year's Address to the Nation*, Prague, January 1, 1990. Available from http://old.hrad.cz/president/Havel/speeches/1990/0101_uk.html (accessed 19 January 2009).

13. *Ibid.*

14. Again, thank you to Prema Srivanasan, who helped with case study.

15. Based on *Fiscal Year 2009 Budget Request to Congress,* Smithsonian Institution.

16. Irvin Molotsky, "President of Fannie Mae to Lead Smithsonian," *New York Times*, September 14, 1999.

17. Elaine Sciolino, "Smithsonian Chief Draws Ire in Making Relics of Old Ways," *New York Times*, July 30, 2001.

18. *Ibid.*

19. James Grimaldi and Jacqueline Trescott, "Secrecy Pervaded Smithsonian on Small's Watch," *Washington Post*, June 21, 2007.

20. Robin Pogrebin, "Senate Panel Admonishes a Beleaguered Smithsonian," *New York Times*, April 12, 2007.

21. Of course, there are numerous examples of individuals who forego large pay packages for positions that satisfy them in other ways, in particular someone in the late stages of his or her career. This fact is not dispositive, merely indicative of further inquiry.

CHAPTER 8

The Common Element—Trust

For it is mutual trust, even more than mutual interest that holds human associations together.

—H. L. MENCKEN

PRISONERS' DILEMMA

For those who are not acquainted with it, the Prisoners' Dilemma is one of the original problems in game theory. Originally developed more than 60 years ago, game theory is an approach to business problem solving and strategic decision making that analyzes the rational choices made by the participants, or players. The important part of game theory is the involvement (and dependency) of each player's actions on one another. The outcome—for you and the other players—will be dependent not only on your decisions, but on the other players or players' decisions. Since the result will depend on the results of all the decisions made, the deciding player must take into account how he expects the other player or players to act.

While the Prisoners' Dilemma has various manifestations, the basic problem is thus: Two suspects are arrested by the police. The police do not have enough hard evidence for a major conviction—only a minor one—and in order to secure a major conviction, the police need to rely on testimony from one of the prisoners. The police separate the two prisoners and visit each of them to offer the same deal: "If you testify for the prosecution against your accomplice and he remains silent, you go free and he receives a full 10-year sentence. If you both remain silent, you both are sentenced to only six months in jail for the minor charge. If you both testify against each other, you will each receive a five-year sentence."

Thus, each prisoner must choose to testify against the other or to remain silent. Each one is assured that the other would not know about the betrayal before the end of the investigation. How should the prisoners act?

The Prisoners' Dilemma is set up as an example where the "best" or "smart" choice for any individual—that is, testifying against the other to avoid the maximum prison sentence—is not the best choice overall. While one might object to the game by noting it is created for this result, the Prisoners' Dilemma has had practical applications in the real world for centuries.[1] Soldiers in battle, since time immemorial, have faced a similar dilemma: "Do I stay and fight and risk death or run away? If I stay and the others flee, I face certain death. If I flee and the others stay, I will live. If we all stay and fight, my risk of death is somewhere between these two extremes."

The rational decision for any one soldier is to flee. While one individual soldier saving his own hide is immaterial, the decision of one soldier to flee has a cascading effect on the whole unit. Commanders have addressed this dilemma in a variety of ways. In ancient Rome, if a soldier saw another soldier abandoning his post, the soldier was required to execute the deserter. If the soldier did not, the soldier who stayed was subject to execution for not executing the deserter. In 1519, Hernán Cortés set out to conquer Mexico. Concerned that some of his men might mutiny and flee back to Cuba instead of facing the Aztec army, he ordered the fleet scuttled[2] to take away the option of retreat. The men no longer had a choice; they had to fight until the end. Through most of military history, the punishment for desertion was death, a punishment designed to take away the incentive to run away.

Yet looking at human behavior, despite huge disincentives, the vast majority of soldiers do not flee and according to some studies,[3] up to 40 percent of individuals who play the Prisoners' Dilemma game choose to remain silent, cooperate, and therefore "win" the game. So how is the Prisoners' Dilemma defeated?

TRUST

The clear optimal result requires risk and trust on the part of all participants. Trust is an incredibly powerful motivator (and distrust a powerful de-motivator) as it forms the basis for all human interaction. Walking across a busy street requires you to trust that drivers will obey the light. Ordering take-out pizza requires a chain of trust that ends in the pizzeria, but starts with farmers and processing plant workers. You trust that the food was properly handled and that the environment was safe. It is a trust not to be taken for granted, as the 2006 *E. coli* outbreak involving spinach and lettuce made abundantly clear.

Trust is hard to quantify, but its impact on our organizations is beyond doubt. Increasing the trust within your organization reduces internal and external costs. Products and services trusted by consumers command price premiums in the marketplace. Moreover, the premium your stock price carries over the market value of your net assets is, to a great degree, a measure of the trust the market places on management's ability to perform well in the future. So while we will discuss trust in terms of interpersonal interactions in other chapters, it is worthwhile to devote some time to discussing the effect of trust on business operations.

Trust reduces risks and uncertainties in transactions between individuals and organizations, in whatever forms those transactions take place.[4] Within your organization, how much of your overhead costs is devoted to oversight, whether that oversight is internal or monitoring vendors? Depending on the industry, between 1 and 6 percent of revenues is devoted to oversight[5]—the more highly regulated the industry or the larger the organization, the higher the percentage.[6] By reducing the risk and uncertainty—the result of increasing internal trust—oversight costs are reduced.

External costs are more apparent and easier to recognize. The idea that an organization incurs transactions costs in the marketplace has been around for over 70 years. In 1937, Ronald Coase published an essay, "The Nature of the Firm," in the academic journal *Economica*. In his essay, Coase outlines the circumstances under which a firm will ascend in the marketplace. He identifies several transactions costs associated with using the market. These costs include information costs (costs associated with finding good prices and determining prices), bargaining costs (costs associated with coming to an agreement with a third party), and enforcement costs (costs associated with making sure the other party lives up to the bargain and enforcing the terms of the contract, if necessary)[7].

THE COST OF TRUST

While trust affects the cost associated with *each* type of transaction, it is simplest for our purposes to discuss enforcement. External events impact the ability (or desire) of a party to complete a contract; yet the majority of enforcement costs deal with the periodic policing of the terms of the transaction. Consider the purchase of a used car. Examine your level of comfort if you were buying the car from (1) your mother, (2) a brother or sister, (3) a friend, (4) a local used-car lot, or (5) a stranger. Individual family nuances aside, the example is meant to point out situations where the trust factor—in the price, in the representations of the condition of the vehicle, in the probability of completion of the deal, and in the ability to redress wrongs—diminishes. Trust reduces the cost of policing and enforcement to nearly zero in the case of buying a car from your mother. The cost is slightly higher when purchasing from your sibling and higher still with a friend. When purchasing from a used-car lot, one trusts that there is some market mechanism in place to temper shifty behavior, though most people would verify the information they receive to the maximum extent possible. As for the last seller—the stranger—this is where the buyer invests the most resources into Coasian transaction costs: researching the fairness of the price, ordering a car history report, getting the car inspected by a trusted mechanic, and other steps to confirm the veracity of the seller's claims.

Further, trust allows sellers to place a premium on the price they charge buyers. Let us continue with the used-car purchase example. You are in the market for a 2006 BMW 330 sedan. Scanning the list of ads, you come across three vehicles of interest. The first is being sold by a private party. The seller represents that the car is in good condition with average mileage and the ad says there is a recent inspection report. It is priced at $24,700. The second car is in the same condition sold by a dealer, which prices the car at $26,100. Finally, you see a similar car being sold by the BMW dealership under its certified pre-owned (CPO) car program. This car lists at $30,800. Which would you choose? According to Edmunds.com, you should be indifferent to these choices as they represent the average fair market value of the cars sold under those circumstances.[8] We can look at this and say that the buyers during this period of time place a $1,400 or 5.6 percent premium on purchasing a car from a dealer rather than a private party. Further, the buyers placed a substantial premium, around $4,600, on purchasing a car through a CPO program.[9] While one may argue that the cache of the BMW name represents a special case, data by Edmunds.com indicates that across all brands, CPO vehicles carry a $1,147 premium compared to non-CPO vehicles.[10] Further, CPO programs are very popular with dealers because of their high profitability. Overall, CPO programs rely on the trust that consumers place in large, established brands and this trust results in a high-profit program.

Of course, a damaged brand can be extremely harmful to the company and its profits. Yet even the most tragic of circumstances, if handled properly, can enhance a company's market stature.

CASE STUDY

THE TYLENOL
POISONINGS

FACTS

On Wednesday morning, September 29, 1982, 12-year-old Mary Kellerman told her mother that she had a headache. Her mother did what millions of Americans would have done; she gave Mary one Extra Strength Tylenol® capsule, a popular pain reliever produced by a subsidiary of Johnson & Johnson. Around the same time and about five miles away, Adam Janus, 27 years old, also took Extra Strength Tylenol for his headache. Mary and Adam died soon thereafter. That evening, as the Janus family gathered to mourn and console each other, Adam's younger brother, Stanley, and Stanley's wife, Theresa, had developed headaches from the stress and confusion of Adam's death. They found Adam's bottle of Tylenol on the kitchen counter and took some. Stanley and Theresa died within 48 hours. On Thursday, Mary Reiner was found dead and on Friday, stewardess Paula Prince was found dead in her apartment. The final victim, Mary McFarland, was killed soon thereafter.

Doctors at the local hospital were suspicious that three family members—all young and in seemingly good health—would die suddenly from natural causes. Originally thought to be carbon monoxide poisoning, toxicology tests soon came back positive for cyanide. With the dosage being 10,000 times higher than killing strength, authorities quickly realized that this was no accident. By a stroke of luck, two off-duty firemen, listening in on the police radios, noticed a common element—the use of Tylenol by the victims. Once the connection to Tylenol was confirmed, Chicago city officials broadcast warnings neighborhood by neighborhood by loudspeaker not to use the product. The Food and Drug Administration (FDA) warned people to avoid Tylenol until the circumstances were understood. What was immediately clear was that the bottles came from different plants and were tampered with once they arrived in five local stores.

Each bottle had some capsules that were laced with cyanide, but only a few. Another bottle—thankfully not yet purchased—was found that contained 14 cyanide-laced capsules out of 50 in the bottle. It seemed the deaths were deliberate and random.

THE ROLE OF LEADERSHIP

Johnson & Johnson's CEO, James E. Burke, was no stranger to difficult situations. In World War II, he commanded an LCT (Landing Craft Tank), an amphibious assault vehicle in the Pacific Theater. After the war, he graduated from the College of the Holy Cross and Harvard Business School. After a few years at Proctor and Gamble, he joined Johnson & Johnson in 1953. Burke was appointed chief executive officer in 1976, but what should have been a capstone to a successful career became a bit of a personal crisis. Burke felt the company had lost its way. In the 1940s, Johnson & Johnson chairman Robert W. Johnson II published the company's "Credo," which states that Johnson & Johnson's first responsibility was to its customers, then to its employees, followed by management, communities, and shareholders. Burke felt strongly connected to the history of Johnson & Johnson and believed that the values expressed through the Credo were critical to the success of the company. Focus on the customer in a "profound and spiritual way," and the rest would take care of itself. Further, Burke had a reputation for ethics. "To me, the old saw is correct," Burke remarked, "that doing good is good business." Burke continued, "[Johnson & Johnson] over 100 years had developed a trusting relationship with the public. Trust is basically what all good trademarks are about."[11]

Under Burke's leadership, the company rediscovered its roots and prospered. By the time of the killings in late 1982, Burke led Johnson & Johnson from $2.5 billion in annual sales to $5.4 billion. When Burke took over as CEO, Tylenol represented 4 percent of the pain reliever market, but by the time of the Chicago killings, the Tylenol brand represented

(Continued)

37 percent of the market for painkillers—outselling Anacin, Bayer, Bufferin, and Excedrin combined—and enjoyed an outstanding reputation in the industry.

On Thursday, September 30, 1982, with the connection between the killings and Tylenol firmly established, that public trust was severely shaken. The company first found out about the deaths that afternoon when a Chicago reporter called the company. The reporter told the Johnson & Johnson public relations department that a medical examiner had just given a press conference saying that people were dying from using Tylenol and the reporter wanted to know if the company had any comment. It was decision time for James Burke. Within an hour, Johnson & Johnson began notifying the Chicago-area press. The company also immediately recalled three batches of product with the lot numbers matching the lots of the bottles used by the victims. By Friday night, the Tylenol killings were the lead story on the national news broadcasts. When Chicago Mayor Jane Byrne announced Prince's death Saturday morning, she also announced a ban on the sale of all Tylenol products. In addition to the city of Chicago, several states, including North Dakota, Colorado, and Massachusetts, took action banning or restricting sales of Tylenol by Saturday.

While McNeil Consumer Products, the Johnson & Johnson subsidiary that manufactures Tylenol, aggressively cooperated with authorities, by Saturday, October 2, it was clear to the leadership at Johnson & Johnson that the company needed to do much more. Burke convened a seven-member strategy team and gave them two marching orders:

First, protect the customer.

Second, save the product.

The public situation continued to deteriorate as panic ensued. Chicago authorities fielded over 700 calls in one day asking about Tylenol. Across the country, people were going into hospitals worried about being poisoned.[12] To complicate matters, the FDA reported over 270 cases of copycat product tampering during the month after the killings. Why anyone would do such a thing was unknown, but what was clear to marketing experts at the time was that Tylenol would not survive.

In addition to the specific recall of the tainted lots, the company pulled all advertising for Tylenol and aggressively sent warnings to health care professionals. Further, the company offered a $100,000 reward for information that led to the capture of the killer.[13] In a subsequent interview,[14] Burke said these decisions were easy to make and were made quickly and without hesitation. The question of what to do with all the Tylenol capsules in stores—more than 30 million bottles—was much tougher. Should the company recall the product? In addition to the financial effect such a recall would have on Johnson & Johnson, executives considered the impact on other companies in the industry. Further, would such a reaction embolden the killer or other copycats to attempt something similar to damage a company or extort money? Burke says that as the strategy team watched the victims buried over the weekend, any concern about the tangential effects of the recall ceased.

Events moved very quickly in the Tylenol poisonings: The first deaths occurred on Wednesday and Tylenol was implicated on Thursday. The nation was alerted on Friday evening and by Saturday morning, with the announcement of Prince's death, it was evident that this could be a major crisis. But, at the time, Burke and his team simply did not know the extent of the problem. The one thing they were reasonably certain about was that the poisoning did not take place while in Johnson & Johnson's control, which was also stated publicly by the Illinois attorney general. This made the temptation to simply defend the company even greater.

But Johnson & Johnson's brand was built on the public trust. Tylenol was promoted with the promise of "safe, fast pain relief." Burke and his team felt strongly that the company's Credo and leadership in the industry demanded that they do more. Johnson & Johnson made the decision to trust

(Continued)

that, if the company did the right thing to protect the customer, the customer, in turn, would reward the company.

On Tuesday, October 5, a decision was made: recall all Tylenol products. The cost to the company was estimated at $125 million. Further, on Thursday, October 7, the company offered to exchange any Tylenol capsule already sold with Tylenol tablets. With those decisions made and in process, Burke and his team were confident they had done everything they could to protect the customer. Only then did they turn their attention to saving the product. What Burke instinctively understood was that by aggressively and publicly putting the safety of the consumer first to the obvious detriment of the bottom line, Johnson & Johnson had already taken the first big step in doing so. At the time of the killings, the market share of Tylenol fell to 8 percent. As a result of its actions and subsequent measures to assure the public that the company was taking steps to make the product tamperproof, Tylenol's share of the pain relief market climbed back over 30 percent.

The manner in which the company handled the two Tylenol poisonings *strengthened* the trust in the company. The decisions made by the management of Johnson & Johnson did not occur in a vacuum or because of some sudden epiphany; they were the result of a dedication to the Credo of Johnson & Johnson by James Burke, the executives, and employees of the company. Further, Mr. Burke's personal leadership and belief in ethics—visible throughout the crises—affirmed the trust the public had in the company.

A Well of Goodwill

Unfortunately, this was not the last time Johnson & Johnson had to deal with product tampering. A similar incident happened in 1986, when a woman in New York died after consuming a cyanide-laced capsule. Faced with similar circumstances, though thankfully only one victim, the company again recalled the Tylenol product and moved aggressively to assure the public that safety came first. With the 1982 murders still relatively fresh in the public minds, it was an open question whether a second poisoning would finally kill the brand. But the public's trust was confirmed in 1982 and reaffirmed by the company's aggressive actions in February 1986. This time, the market share of Tylenol dropped only into the low 20 percent and was nearly fully recovered in five months.

As tragic as the circumstances were in Chicago in 1982 and New York in 1986, the Tylenol killings are not a unique situation. There have been several disasters affecting organizations that have had a significant impact on the lives of consumers and the companies. In the early 1970s, the Ford Pinto was alleged to have a design defect that could cause the gas tank to explode in the event of a rear-end collision. In 1979, the feedwater pumps at Three Mile Island Reactor 2 failed, resulting in a partial core meltdown and the release of radioactive krypton and iodine-131. Later in 1979, American Airlines Flight 191 lost a wing engine upon takeoff from Chicago's O'Hare International Airport killing 271 people on board plus two additional people on the ground. In 1984, in Bhopal, India, an accident at a plant jointly owned by Union Carbide and Indian interests released a toxic cloud of gas that killed several thousand people. In 1989, the *Exxon Valdez* struck a reef and spilled nearly 11 million gallons of crude oil into Alaska's Prince William Sound. In 1999, Coca-Cola faced a similar crisis when school children in Europe fell ill after consuming Coca-Cola, resulting in a national recall of the soft drink in Belgium, France, the Netherlands, and Luxembourg.

In each instance, the reaction of the company and the public show how difficult it is to maintain the public trust. In the case of the Tylenol killings, the reaction of the company has become the standard to which all others are held. One would think that since Johnson & Johnson's reaction to the Tylenol poisonings was universally praised by consumers, media, and the punditry that other corporations would model their behavior on the executives at Johnson & Johnson. Yet that is not the case, and a good example of failure to maintain the public trust is the Firestone–Ford Tire recalls.

FACTS

In August 2000, Firestone recalled over 6 million tires be-cause of an alleged defect that caused sport utility vehicles to roll over. The problems faced by Firestone are similar to the Tylenol incident in that they involved a product—tires—with an essential public safety function. In the 1970s, the Firestone 500 radial tire was implicated in 34 deaths due to tread separation. Unlike the Tylenol incident, where the trag-edy occurred suddenly and was seemingly random, the problem of tread separation was known internally at Fire-stone and by the automobile manufacturers, who did work together to find a solution eventually. In March 1978, the Na-tional Highway and Transportation Safety Administration (NHTSA) began a formal investigation, and Firestone's initial reaction was one of noncooperation. Yet by October 1978, Firestone was forced to recall nearly 9 million tires at a cost of $150 million.[15] The revelations of the investigations by the government and the press painted the company in a very negative light, severely eroding public trust in the prod-uct and the company.

Then in the late 1990s, reports surfaced of problems with Firestone's Wilderness AT tires on Ford Explorer sport utility vehicles. The company faced a similar problem with tire in-tegrity, but the loss of tire integrity on an SUV could have devastating consequences, including causing a rollover. The initial reports were coming from warm-weather areas, such as Venezuela and Saudi Arabia, and Ford immediately began replacing tires in the affected areas. Firestone resisted replacing the tires, seeking further data based on Firestone's study of tires in Arizona, Texas, and Nevada. Ford used Fire-stone data to pinpoint the problem to a specific tire manu-facturing plant. Firestone began using replacement tires from other plants, including Bridgestone, Firestone's new parent company, plants in Japan. The NHTSA requested

Firestone to recall another 1.4 million tires. Firestone re-fused. In the end, over 150 deaths and 500 injuries have been reputed to have been caused by the failure.[16]

THE ROLE OF LEADERSHIP

Even with the experience of their 1978 recall and the exam-ple of Johnson & Johnson before them, Firestone manage-ment resisted addressing the problem aggressively. Fundamentally, the management team saw the problem as one of engineering, not public trust. One Firestone executive was reputed to say that Firestone has got such a high vol-ume of tires that looking for the root cause is like looking for a needle in a haystack. This response exemplifies an engineer's tin ear to the issue of consumer safety and does nothing to assure the buying public that the company can fix the problem or that it *cares* about safety.

Ford Motor Company's response also fell short and sus-tained collateral damage as a consequence. Ford immediately pointed the finger at Firestone and aggressively tried to dem-onstrate that Firestone tires failed at a higher rate than tires from other manufacturers; in response, Firestone pointed out that Wilderness AT tires performed as expected with other vehicles. Ford chief executive officer Jacques Nasser was the face of the company during the crisis and attempted to assure the public that Ford bore no responsibility for the deaths. Both companies traded accusations of the other's culpability and provided data to support their claims. While Ford did do and say many of the right things, CEO Nasser, as the face of Ford during the crisis, came across as combative and took a harsh tone in interviews.[17] In the publicly broadcast Congressional hearings, Nasser does not come across well, at one point seeming to question data Representative Tauzin presents as "data that you have that no one else seems to have."[18] As facts leaked out that were damaging to both companies, each became more aggressive in its defense. In the end, a nearly 100-year relationship between Ford and Firestone was severed and both brands were tarnished.

(*Continued*)

While it is difficult to calculate the actual long-term effect of the recall on the Ford brand and Explorer sales because of the drastic impact of September 11 on the business environment, we can see the near-term impact that the recall had on the Explorer's market position. The Explorer held between 25 percent and 30 percent of the midsize SUV market during most of the 1990s. In 1999, the Ford Explorer held just over 25 percent of the market and Ford Motor Company posted record profits for an American car company. By the end of 2000, the Explorer held just 19 percent of the market.

Beyond the figures for the Explorer, we can look at the thrust of the messaging Ford was sending to the public. In the early 1980s, in response to a reputation for less than perfect quality, Ford launched the "Quality is Job 1" ad campaign. For 17 years, Ford reiterated that point to the buying public. In 1998, Ford replaced "Quality is Job 1" with a $40 million per year "Better Ideas. Driven by You." advertising campaign.[19] Ford did so confident in the fact that it had improved vehicle quality and had closed the gap with the Japanese automobile manufacturers. Then, after years of brand building, Ford refused to take any responsibility for the tires on its vehicles. A position of trust with the public that took many years and millions and millions of dollars to build was severely damaged.

Two Approaches

The lessons of the Johnson & Johnson Tylenol killings and the Firestone recalls can be summed up as follows.

First, trust is established or reestablished with honest and transparent communications. And trust is the most important element in surviving a corporate crisis. The facts will come out at some point. Attempts to hide information or be less than forthcoming are bound to backfire. Johnson & Johnson proactively responded to the crisis while Firestone (and later Ford) suppressed information. James

Burke's public concern did much to build trust when the company needed it; Jacques Nasser's stubborn refusal to accept any responsibility had the opposite effect.

Second, the speed at which a company addresses issues affects trust. Ultimately, businesses succeed by convincing complete strangers to hand over their hard-earned dollars for a product. Johnson & Johnson zealously protected those consumers in a time of crisis. Despite the public pronouncements, Firestone and Ford seemed more concerned with blaming each other than to the consumers. In the case of Ford, the company did act quickly to protect the consumer, but that message was lost in the blame game. Now, it is clear that businesses need to create value for stakeholders other than the customer, but if customers lose trust in the company and the product, all other stakeholders will ultimately suffer.

Finally, the public spotlight exaggerates the effects of a company's actions and multiplies the creation or destruction of trust. Johnson & Johnson was clearly concerned about the image of the company and product but recognized that, until the immediate crisis past, spinning the situation would be unseemly. Johnson & Johnson took steps to make the Tylenol tampering an industry issue: "There but for the grace of God goes . . . Excedrin," for example. After the recall and exchange, it made the solution an industry issue. Firestone and Ford chose to narrowly define the problem as the fault of the other when, in fact, they could have framed it as an industry issue to be solved together or with new technology, such as tire pressure monitors that, at that point, were only offered on high-end vehicles. It would be difficult for competitors to fight against a simple safety improvement.

Bringing this full circle, let's return to the Prisoners' Dilemma with which we opened this chapter. If we examine the strategies of the two players we have discussed in this chapter, Johnson & Johnson and Firestone and Ford, it is clear that James Burke and the Johnson & Johnson team prudently avoided the false choice embodied by the Prisoners' Dilemma, make sure you save yourself first, while Firestone and Ford succumbed to it.

Ultimately, in their roles as players in the Prisoners' Dilemma, each company was faced with a choice to place itself at greater potential risk by trusting that the other player—the customer—would reward it. Johnson & Johnson, relying on its corporate history, its Credo, and the firm conviction of its CEO, cast its lot with the customer. Its gamble paid off for both. Firestone and Ford selected the rational choice—self-preservation—and lost not only a 100-year-old business relationship, but also lost the confidence—and trust—of the marketplace.

■ NOTES

1. In Plato's early dialogue *Laches*, Socrates discusses courage in the context of the soldiers' dilemma.
2. In some accounts, Cortés burned the fleet in front of the men.
3. Amos Tversky, *Preference, Belief, and Similarity: Selected Writings* (Cambridge, MA: MIT Press, 2003), 712.
4. This is not *blind trust*. Trust is built on the principles described later in this book.
5. See, for example, RAND Corporation research for the Department of Defense on Acquisition Reform.
6. It should be noted that start-ups are infamous for having low oversight costs and, consequently, being nimble and adaptable. But the high rate of failure of new ventures suggests the utility of at least some oversight.
7. Coase, and other early theorists, in particular Professor Frank Knight, also address risk and uncertainty in the development of the firm. One could argue that this is a transaction cost between parties that may be reduced by "trust." To do so at length would require a lesson and an analysis of transactions cost economics (TCE) in the modern sense and a "translation" of these inexact terms (*trust*, *risk*, and *uncertainty*) into the lexicon used by TCE economist, such as Oliver Williamson and his proponents and detractors. That is a task for another day.
8. Report of a 2006 BMW 330i sedan with 35,000 miles and no additional options for the Boston, Massachusetts, area in September 2008.
9. The exact amount of the premium related to trust is imprecise. The $4,800 additional includes some limited warranty and other services that represent a portion of the premium. In the instant case, BMW offers a limited two-year/50,000-mile warranty and services related to roadside assistance, lockout, and towing. While individual circumstances, such as AAA

membership, may offset the value of some services which further complicates the "value" of these latter additional services, it is clear that the BMW warranty carries some not insignificant premium over a private party and third party dealer.

10. Kate McLeod, "Certified Pre-Owned Gains Traction with Buyers," *Edmunds.com*. Available from http://www.edmunds.com/advice/buying/articles/123823/article.html (accessed 20 January 2008).

11. Daniel F. Cuff, "Making a Difference; Looking for Good Deeds," *New York Times*, February 9, 1992.

12. At the dosage found in the tainted capsules, a victim would not have time to make a call. Death was certain within minutes of consumption.

13. To this date, the killer remains unknown.

14. Rick Atkinson, "The Tylenol Nightmare: How a Corporate Giant Fought Back," *Kansas City Times*, November 12, 1982.

15. In the interest of fairness, it should be noted that Firestone did not ignore the problem. Once it became apparent that the defect was a result of design flaws, Firestone did its best to remedy the flaws in the process. Yet despite Firestone's efforts to solve the problem, Firestone was clearly not as transparent or forthcoming as Johnson & Johnson.

16. Any figures should be viewed with caution, given the difficulty of ascertaining the exact cause of an automobile accident. Further, the legal stakes involved give each side an incentive to maximize or minimize deaths related to tire failure.

17. Tim Burt, "On the Record and Off the Record with Ford CEO Jac Nasser," *Financial Times*, October 18, 2000.

18. Kwame Holman, "Congressional Tire Investigation," *The News Hour with Jim Lehrer*, June 19, 2001.

19. In 1998, Ford Motor Company spent $2.2 billion on advertising.

CHAPTER 9

Building an Army of Davids

One man with courage makes a majority.

—ANDREW JACKSON

HERDING CATS

In earlier chapters, we examined the "whys" of unethical or deviant behavior and the influences on behavior of individual circumstances, group dynamics, and the role of leadership in setting the tone and validating the environment. Our focus had been why the system breaks down. Then, in Chapter 8, we started discussing the foundation for creating a system that does not break down by examining the critical element of trust in the workings of any organization. In the next few chapters, we discuss how to structure your organization to minimize the risk of unethical behavior.

We start out with a few caveats. First, it is not necessary to have every employee in your organization act like a Kool-Aid-swilling zealot. That is neither possible nor necessary. The objective is to build enough active and passive support for common goals to efficiently achieve your strategic objectives. Ethical behavior should be a given, but with enough support in the organization, any and all *unethical* behavior will not be tolerated at any level.

The second caveat is that the following are meant to be generalizations that you, as business leaders, can tailor to your organization and its strategic objectives. How these ideas manifest themselves in an industrial organization of 10,000 employees, a technology company of 1,000 employees, or a not-for-profit charity of 80 will be different and rightfully so. We have tried to stay abstract enough where your understanding of the concepts and your organization should make the implementation path evident.

I SAMUEL I7

In 2006, blogger and University of Tennessee law professor Glenn Reynolds wrote a book called *An Army of Davids: How Markets and Technology Empower Ordinary People to Beat Big Media, Big Government, and Other Goliaths.*[1] Reynolds's proposition is that the power of technology is changing the power allocation in society away from large entities—big media, big government, and the rest—to small entities, including individuals. Reynolds, the man behind the popular blog Instapundit, focuses on the ability of the individual to use technology to bring about change. While the availability of the Internet may enable more rapid change than in years past, motivated individuals have brought about change against powerful interests throughout history. The Protestant Reformation, with the aid of that new fangled printing press technology, took on the Catholic Church. The Abolitionists in England boycotted sugar to hurt Caribbean slave trading interests. Dissidents in the Soviet bloc used *samizdat*, a technique that harkened back to the days prior to the printing press, to affect democratic change. These historical causes, as well as the examples Reynolds cites, are a small set of examples of creating organizations that drive results through principles that allow motivated individuals to do great things.

Despite what may seem like a bleak picture painted in the prior chapters, your organization and its relationship to its employees starts out in a positive manner. As an employee enters an organization, he or she arrives with skills, ambitions, and a desire to do a good job. The organization has a need to fill and find the person qualified to meet that need. The employer and employee relationship starts out filled with promise. From the organization's perspective, building on that promise and preventing ethical lapses requires that the organization take advantage of the fact that the employee resides on the social sphere and that it satisfies the deficiency needs of the employee by building trust.

Recall that the majority of employees will operate primarily on the social sphere, that is, their propensity to act in a certain manner will be driven by a desire to be accepted and liked by others. The work environment presents a unique gathering of individuals there by necessity—financial opportunity—rather than by choice. As a counter example, your circle of friends constitutes a group where you may be liked and respected, but you are there by choice. Other associations become either one of choice or convenience. Civic or church groups are examples of associations of choice, while work is typically one of necessity. The goal of the organization is to change that relationship to one of choice. To do this, the organization must develop a clear "cause" and promote in its employees a belief in and desire to achieve its "cause." In doing so, the organization creates a desire to be part of the organization beyond the financial aspect of income. While this will never overcome the monetary incentive, it will provide a positive, additional incentive to come to work, and employees that are engaged in the organization are your best defense against unethical behavior.

BREAKING THE CHAINS

It is difficult to convey the enormity of the task facing the awkwardly named the Society for the Abolition of the Slave Trade upon its formation in 1787.[2] While slavery was illegal on English soil, the trade of slaves from West Africa to the Caribbean and Americas had been big business[3] since 1562. The supply of slave labor to the plantations of the Caribbean and Southern United States was seen as critical to the production of sugar, tobacco, rice, and other staples. Local cities, such as Manchester, England, supplied trading stuff, such as cloth to the slave traders to exchange for human cargo. A significant percentage of English Parliamentarians had a vested financial interest in the continued success of this vile business.[4]

If the business interests were not enough of an obstacle, 9 of the 12 of the founders of the Society for the Abolition of the Slave Trade were Quakers. While possessing indubitable integrity, the Quakers were viewed as a bit, to put it kindly, out of the mainstream to the point that they were debarred from standing for Parliament. The original 12 made for an odd group, but through effort to inform the public, and English women in particular, began to attract more members and members with considerably more influence, including Member of Parliament William Wilberforce and potter Josiah Wedgwood. The Society called upon the personal experiences of former slaves and former slave ship captain John Newton, famous for authoring the hymn *Amazing Grace,* to bring to light to a public that was ignorant of the practices of the slave trade. The Society used pamphlets, medallions, boycotts of Caribbean sugar, petitions, and other methods to raise public awareness. The moral and statistical arguments slowly gained proponents both active and passive in Parliament, including two future Prime Ministers, William Pitt and William Grenville. Led by Wilberforce, the English Abolitionists managed to maintain momentum during the French Revolutionary Wars and the Napoleonic Wars to pass the law abolishing the slave trade in 1807 and, finally, slavery itself was abolished in the British Empire in 1833.

BASIC PRINCIPLES

Most organizations will not be confused with the Society for the Abolition of the Slave Trade anytime soon, but there is no reason to take the cause metaphor to that level. Instead, your organization should focus on vision, mission, and values. Quick question: What are your organization's mission, vision, and values? If you cannot articulate your vision, mission, and values, your organization has not done the basic work in creating a unifying "cause." The underlying idea animating your organization's vision, mission, and values combine to create the "cause" of the organization. The vision, mission, and values are the what, why, and how behind your organization.

It is not this book's immediate purpose to walk you through a vision, mission, and values exercise, but it is important to understand what we mean. We have discussed in prior chapters, the IBM values that are articulated upfront in the "About Us" page on IBM's Web site, and in the Tylenol Case Study, the Johnson & Johnson Credo plays a critical role in guiding the response of the management to the crisis. It is clear that each was developed in accordance to the needs of that organization. The vision is the ultimate purpose of the organization. By "purpose," the focus is on what constitutes long-term market success, so that while the purpose may be "to make a boatload of money," to do so requires a success in the marketplace that should be articulated. For example, the vision of the National Education Association (NEA) is "a great public school for every student."[5] Concise and simple, the NEA's vision is easily understood and lofty enough to inspire members.

The mission statement is why the organization exists and wants to achieve its vision. The mission statement may be short or long, but should directly relate to the business. Nike's mission statement is "to bring inspiration and innovation to every athlete in the world,"[6] which serves as the nexus between vision and values. For FedEx Corporation, its mission statement is more comprehensive:

> FedEx will produce superior financial returns for its shareowners by providing high value-added logistics, transportation and related information services through focused operating companies. Customer requirements will be met in the highest quality manner appropriate to each market segment served. FedEx Corporation will strive to develop mutually rewarding relationships with its employees, partners, and suppliers. Safety will be the first

consideration in all operations. Corporate activities will be conducted to the highest ethical and professional standards.[7]

The values, of course, are the "how": What ideals drive the business? These are the personal qualities the organization expects from each employee and should directly relate to the business objectives. Wal-Mart has three: respect for the individual, service to our customers, and striving for excellence.[8] While not called values, these are the underlying tenets that drive Wal-Mart's purpose of "saving people money, so they can live better."[9]

The most difficult challenge in determining vision, mission, and values is often drawing the line between what is a vision and mission— or the idea that we need the word "integrity" in our values statements because it looks good. Nonsense. Distinctions are unimportant. Note how FedEx incorporates all elements in its mission statement. Johnson & Johnson calls their principle a Credo. What matters is defining the cause in a way that connects the organization. The vision of the United States Army is expressed in its primary field manual, *FM 1*:

> The Nation has entrusted the Army with preserving its peace and freedom, defending its democracy, and providing opportunities for its Soldiers to serve the country and personally develop their skills and citizenship. Consequently, we are and will continuously strive to remain among the most respected institutions in the United States. To fulfill our solemn obligation to the Nation, we must remain the preeminent land power on earth-the ultimate instrument of national resolve; strategically dominant on the ground where our Soldiers' engagements are decisive.[10]

No matter what they are called or how many words are used, the final result needs to connect your organization with its employees, stakeholders, and market.

EVANGELIZE

The first test of the usefulness of your values, mission, and vision "cause" is the enthusiasm of senior leadership in evangelizing the principles. If your leadership team does not buy it, your organization will not either. This will be a recurring theme in the next few chapters: Leadership needs to live, eat, sleep, and breathe every effort to promote ethical conduct in the organization. If they are unwilling to do so, then the cause will be lost and resources wasted. A lack of effort to espouse guiding principles will also indicate one of two things: your organization needs new principles or your organization needs new leadership.

Effective evangelization means two primary courses of action. The first is to ensure that the organization tenets are integrated into the processes and operations. Done properly, this will provide a consistent messaging to your organization. If customer service is a core part of the corporate cause, do the policies in place promote superlative customer service? If trust is a core value, how much trust do your policies allow? Policies and procedures that do not consider or reflect the vision, mission, and values of the organization are a common obstacle to creating an engaged employee. The challenge lies in translating the loftiness of the corporate values to mundane tasks. By way of example, the values of the American Heart Association (AHA) are: Integrity, Inclusiveness, Dedication, Excellence, Sensitivity, and Vision. Now the truth of the matter is that it is simply impossible to have every policy and procedure at the AHA directly and obviously tie to each of those values. This is fine. But care must be taken to ensure that the policies and procedures do not go against your organization's values.

The second course of action is to ensure that employees' behavior, senior leadership's in particular, reflect and reinforce the principles of the organization. While it may not be apparent on the face as to how to make an accounts receivable write-off policy consistent with the corporate vision, the behavior of the employees is easier to observe. Further, incentives can be created, such as tying in corporate values into a performance review. Did the head of sales meet his or her goals while embodying the company's principles? The incorporation of behavior that promotes the organization's cause should be a mandatory part of the evaluation process. The immediate focus, as you may imagine, are individuals in positions of trust: executives and managers, human resources, finance, legal, and others depending on your organization. Further, the more visible the position, the more critical the employee in that position embodies the vision, mission, and values of the organization.

The goal of this action is to create a setting that is attractive to the employee in a manner that instills the employee with a desire to be engaged with the organization. If done correctly, the employee will speak well of the organization, plan to stay at the organization, and will look for ways to make the organization better. In other words, the employee, by embracing the cause, will seek acceptance and admiration of the group, which matches their social sphere profile.

CASE STUDY   JORDAN'S FURNITURE[11]

If you reside in the eastern Massachusetts or southern New Hampshire area, you know Jordan's Furniture. More accurately, you know Barry and Eliot Tatelman[12] and their unique approach to furniture retailing. Taking over from their father in the early 1970s, the brothers quickly sought to imprint their own ideas and personalities on the business. Their first big idea was to have fun. As Barry tells it, "At Jordan's Furniture, the single most telling characteristic of our culture is that Eliot and I want to have fun, and we want our employees and customers to have fun as well. One way to do that is by injecting humor into our advertising. Since most of our hallmark television commercials feature Eliot and me, we use our personalities to amuse and attract customers."[13] In the early 1970s, all Jordan's had was a limited print advertising budget. Barry and Eliot shifted their ad dollars to radio and started a series of quirky, humorous radio and, later on, television skits depicting Barry and Eliot in all manner of situations, all reinforcing the notion of fun.

While Barry and Eliot were having fun, the word "fun" is not known to be associated with furniture shopping. In 1987, Jordan's opened its third store in Avon, Massachusetts, which featured MOM, or Motion Odyssey Movie, which takes place in a 48-seat theater with a four-story movie screen. All the proceeds from this $2.5 million investment go to charity. In 1998, Jordan's Natick opened with its virtual reality game, Bourbon Street, Kelly's Roast Beef, and an IMAX 3D theater. And, yes, you can buy furniture there.

And buy people did. In the past 25 years, Jordan's grew from 15 employees to over 1,200 employees, with sales of over a quarter of a billion dollars. Statistically, Jordan's numbers are impressive. In an industry where inventory turn averages one to two times per year, Jordan's turns its inventory 13 times per year. There are no promotional sales at the main stores. Despite the investment in the famous TV ads, Jordan's marketing and advertising spend is 70 percent lower than other furniture retailers. Most impressively, Jordan's averages sales of $950 per square foot whereas most furniture retailers average sales of $150 per square foot—they have the highest in the country according to the trade publication *Furniture Today*.

The most critical element, according to Barry, was the employees. The J-Team, as they are called, embraces the culture of fun. The sales staff is not paid commission, but earns a salary, alleviating the pressure tactics and aligning the goals of the employee and customer. New employees get their first taste of corporate culture when Barry and Eliot join them for a casual welcome dinner enforcing the importance of each employee and their connection with the owners. There are "Fun Days" throughout the year with barbecues, mini-bingo, and ice cream buffets. Managers and supervisors reward high performers with lunches on a Friday afternoon and the company sponsors a corporate-wide party every year or two.

(Continued)

But the party that garnered the most amount of attention occurred on May 10, 1999, when Jordan's flew every employee, filling four chartered planes, from Boston to Bermuda for a beach party. The group occupied a terminal at Logan's International Airport and was the largest single-event departure in the airport's history. In Bermuda, games, water activities, and tours awaited the employees and Bermuda rolled out the red carpet for the company. The event, which started at 3:00 AM did not end with the early evening flight back to Boston. The next day, a breakfast buffet awaited the employees at the stores and Barry and Eliot went to each location to shake hands and thank the employees once again. Later that year, Warren Buffett's Berkshire Hathaway purchased Jordan's Furniture, resulting in a tidy sum for the brothers . . . and the employees. Barry and Eliot bonused each employee $0.50 for every hour worked in the company or approximately $1,000 for every year of service.

The lesson from Jordan's is not to shower your employees with money or to throw pizza parties on a regular basis. Jordan's success resulted from the creation of an *organization cause* promoted and endorsed by the leadership and embraced by employees who, by their individual efforts, produced an extraordinarily high-performing organization. This cause was consistently maintained and applied to the business over a period of years.

BACK TO MASLOW

Kohlberg's moral development model (discussed in Chapter 5) and its findings are only one side of the equation. While the vast majority of individuals seek satisfying social interactions, each experiences pressures along the way. Stresses and pressure become critical when they are due to a needs deficiency relating to basic needs, in particular financial security. Now it is quite clear that there is only so much an organization can do to help the employees with personal issues, but the organization does have responsibility to minimize unnecessary pressure at work. Note the word "unnecessary." It is utopian fantasy to think that your organization will be stress free,[14] but pressure to perform comes in different forms. In the Walt Pavlo case study in Chapter 5, the situation deteriorated rapidly after his superiors set an unattainable target for bad debt expense: $15 million rather than the recommended figure of $180 million. In that situation, Pavlo was immediately faced with a catch-22, with both outcomes being disastrous.

For an organization, the biggest financial stress an employee feels relates to the loss of their job. Disappointment may come from a small raise or bonus, but, for most employees, this all pales in comparison to sudden job loss. Now job loss is a part of the corporate landscape and, quite frankly, it is important for any organization to be able to dismiss employees who do not perform to acceptable standards. Where the fear of job loss acts against the interest of the organization is when there is retaliation or other circumstances where it is in the interests of the organization for the employee to pursue a course of action, but the employee fears that in doing so, their job is in jeopardy.

In addition to situations where the employee is forced to leave involuntarily, there are circumstances where the smart long-term answer to a dilemma is to resign. An employee in Pavlo's situation could have quit and endured some short-term stress of finding a new job. From a personal perspective, that was clearly the right thing to do, but from an organization perspective, if the only option an employee has when faced with a dilemma is to quit, then the organization is seriously dysfunctional and has the same effect as an involuntary termination. Such an employee should have had the option of reporting the circumstances to leadership through alternative means (such as internal audit), or to the CFO, or other senior executive, or anonymously, but unless the employee feels they will be supported when the whistle is blown, they simply will not do so. An employee facing such a dilemma confronts an enormous psychological obstacle, but in both instances, the fear is the same: "I am going to lose my job." Fear, anger, and resentment follow, circumstances that can lead to unethical behavior.

MORAL HAZARD

Pavlo's dilemma was the result of a moral hazard created by MCI. The idea of moral hazard originated in the insurance industry where insurers faced a balancing act of how much to charge for the risk insured against. At some point, the price will get so low that the insured may not take due care of the property, knowing that if something went wrong, they would be compensated for the loss regardless. In the credit crisis that occurred in late 2008, moral hazard was used to describe the idea that the individuals who originated the mortgage loans—and who enjoyed the economic benefit of the origination— did not have to worry about consequences if the loan went bad months or years later. Further, moral hazard objections to the various bailouts—of banks, AIG, the automobile manufacturers—all were premised on the notion that people who behaved irresponsibly or poorly were being "rewarded"[15] at the expense of those homeowners and companies who have been prudent.

For our immediate purposes, moral hazard should be taken to mean the dissociation of authority and responsibility and this represents the most common and most dangerous ethical risk organizations face. While we have and will discuss many aspects of business ethics, if you take away only one thing it should be that anytime someone in your organization has responsibility for the outcome, but is not empowered with the authority to determine the outcome, the chance for unethical behavior increases dramatically.

This is readily apparent in the Pavlo case. Pavlo did not have the authority to address the amount of bad debt in his area but was responsible for the consequences of a decision so removed from reality there was simple no legitimate way the issue can be reconciled. This is not meant to justify the behavior; rather it is meant to point out the root cause: If management had acted on Pavlo's recommendation the story would have had a very different ending. While an extreme example, it concisely points out the problems that arise under this form of moral hazard.

A few things should be noted about this problem. The first is that the employee with the responsibility, Pavlo in the instant case, does not have to have sole responsibility for the outcome. Had Pavlo taken a different path and the bad debt house of cards collapsed under its own weight, there would surely have been others being held accountable, possibly including the managers who made the decision not to address the bad debt problem. But it was made clear to Pavlo, and clear in his mind, that he was to find a solution and he was responsible for addressing the problem.

In addition, actual responsibility is not necessary, only the reasonable perception and belief in responsibility. One might argue that it is clear that if events had taken their course and the bad debt problem come to a head, that Pavlo's actions—raising the issue and suggesting that it be immediately addressed—would have covered his posterior. This is difficult to know, but it is clear that Pavlo was under the distinct, and reasonable, impression that he was responsible for solving the problem to achieve the goals his superiors outlined and he would be blamed for any failure.

Finally, and this should be obvious, the authority the employee has must be directly applicable to the responsibility assumed. If not, the organization faces the danger of focused authority; that is, when the employee attempts to solve the problem, he or she is responsible for utilizing *only* what power they have. If that authority does not directly relate to solving the problem, there is a danger that the employee will utilize the authority in a manner that exacerbates the problem or covers the employee's tracks. Pavlo certainly had a certain amount of authority and gained knowledge that he used to further his fraud. In his case, he knew loopholes in the accounting and auditing function that allowed him to disguise his transactions. To address this moral hazard requires that an organization and its employees clearly understand the lines of authority and creates a mechanism for addressing situations where there is a mismatch. The specifics of the mechanism to avert this moral hazard will vary from organization to organization but will center on effective managers and alternative communication channels.

Emphasizing people skills and training are important to developing the right managers and hotlines, ombudsmen, open-door policies, or other initiatives that will develop alternative communication channels. However, if open communications is seen by your employees as a tool rather than part of the culture of the organization, the effectiveness of any program will be limited. Barry and Eliot Tatelman of Jordan's Furniture built an employee culture based on fun and openness and made it work because everyone in the organization believed that they meant it. It is certain that not every employee at Jordan's was happy, but, true to its motto, Barry and Eliot created and reinforced an environment where Jordan's was not just a store, but an experience.

Causes and Culture

In Chapter 5, we examined what causes an individual to make unethical decisions. We found that a person's moral development put them in the social sphere or moral framework where being liked and respected by others is a prime motivation for behavior. With this in mind, organizations should develop an environment that exploits this motivation by using its vision, mission, and values to develop an organizational "cause" to attract the right type of employee and encourage them to perform in an exemplary manner. An organizational cause that is reinforced by the culture, environment, and actions of leadership will develop an employee base that is fully engaged with the organization. Employees who are fully engaged will speak well of the organization and promote the organization to others, plan to stay at the organization, and will look for ways to make the organization better, more efficient, and more profitable.

The vision, mission, and values of the organization may be evergreen or dynamic, but should authentically represent the organization and its goals. It is important not to worry about having a vision and a mission and no fewer than five, and no more than seven, articulated

values. No two organizations are the same, so there is no canned answer. Rather, the goal is to find and describe the core tenets that drive
the business. Start small if necessary, but once defined, care must be
taken to make certain policies and procedures explicitly match the
principles where possible and in no way proscribe actions or incent
behavior inconsistent with the organizational principles.

As powerful as a corporate cause can be, it will be undone if
employees are stressed and pressured to compromise those principles.
The most common and most dangerous ethical risk organizations face
is the moral hazard represented by the dissociation of authority and
responsibility. Where employees are forced to assume the consequences of action, but are not empowered with the proper authority
to pursue a course of action consistent with the organization's principles, the situation can easily deteriorate into one where ethics are
compromised. Addressing this dilemma requires that an organization
and its employees clearly understand the lines of authority and that
the organization creates a mechanism for addressing situations where
there is a mismatch.

In this chapter, we have examined the individual employee and
discussed the dynamic between the employee and the organization
from the employee's point of view. That is only half of the story. The
organization has a number of options to create group dynamics to
further reduce the chance of behavior that is unacceptable and to
encourage behavior that enhances corporate performance and
reputation.

■ NOTES

1. Glenn Reynolds, *An Army of Davids: How Markets and Technology Empower
   Ordinary People to Beat Big Media, Big Government, and Other Goliaths* (New
   York: Thomas Nelson, 2006).
2. For a powerful account of the English Abolitionist movement, see Adam
   Hochschild, *Bury the Chains, The British Struggle to Abolish Slavery* (London:
   Macmillan, 2005).
3. The value of the slaves traded during the late eighteenth and early nine-
   teenth centuries is difficult to translate into current dollars, but 12.5 million

slaves were involved and the approximate price of a male slave in South Carolina in the late eighteenth century was $300. Using a rough inflator, the value runs into the tens of billions of today's dollars.

4. Slavery, tragically, is still big business: The International Labor Organization estimates some 2.5 million persons are in some form of bondage in any given year, with global trafficking estimated to be valued at $32 billion. Eighty percent of the victims are women. (Source: "A Horrible Business," *The Economist*, June 14, 2008.)

5. National Education Association, "About," *NEA.org*. Available from http://www.nea.org/home/2580.htm (accessed 20 January 2009).

6. Nike Corp., "Company Overview: If you have a body, you are an athlete," *NikeID*. Available from http://www.nikebiz.com/company_overview/index.html (accessed 20 January 2009).

7. FedEx Corp., "Mission Statement," *Investor Relations*. Available from http://ir.fedex.com/documentdisplay.cfm?DocumentID=125 (accessed 20 January 2009).

8. Wal-Mart Stores, Inc., "3 Basic Beliefs & Values." Available from http://walmartstores.com/AboutUs/321.aspx (accessed 20 January 2009).

9. *Ibid.*

10. United States Army, Chapter 2, Section 2-23, in *FM 1*.

11. Thank you to Roberto Scalese for researching the background for this case study.

12. Ninety-five percent of New Englanders also know them as Barry and Eliot—no last name required.

13. Barry Tatelman, "You Can't Take That Away from Us," *Entrepreneurship.org*. Available from http://www.entrepreneurship.org/Resources/Detail/Default.aspx?id=10676 (accessed 20 January 2009).

14. Nor would it be advisable to be stress free. Pressure can produce positive results by developing new thinking and approaches.

15. *Reward* is not meant to imply that those responsible did not endure some hardship—loss of reputation, unemployment, fines—only that the "bailouts" envisioned some safety net for the companies involved.

CHAPTER 10

The Positive Power of Peer Pressure

Every man has a mob self and an individual self, in varying proportions.

—D. H. LAWRENCE

THE GENTLEMAN AT DINNER[1]

At a city sports award dinner, four couples sat down at the same table. The seating arrangements accommodated 10 people, so there was room for two additional people. Several minutes later, another couple ventured over to take the vacant seats. Introductions were exchanged and drinks ordered. The original four couples were in their thirties and forties and all had children in the various sports programs. The late arrivers were older, most likely in their early seventies.

Time passed and the older woman excused herself to go to the ladies room. As she stood, her husband also stood and remained standing until she left table. When she returned, again the gentleman stood as she sat down. Soon after that, two women from the first group also left to use the powder room. The older gentleman once again stood. This time the other men at the table stole glances at each other not quite sure what to do. By the time the two women returned, as the older gentlemen stood, the four other men also stood. For the remainder of the evening, much to the enjoyment of the women, the younger men continued to not only stand, but became quite conscious of their manners and etiquette. At no time did the older gentlemen say anything, nor did the women insist on the behavior, but a pattern just developed—at least for that evening. This story illustrates in a simple way how group behavior can be modified quickly and provides the start of a framework for understanding how organizations can use group dynamics in a positive manner that promotes ethical behavior and drive performance.

Now recall from Chapter 6, that the chances that an individual will conform to the behavior of the group are determined by four elements that were derived from theories of social control. Social control theory, based on the work of Travis Hirschi, was derived as an explanation for *deviant behavior*, being defined as behavior outside the expectations of the group. The weakening of the social bonds increases the risk of abnormal behavior and, because of this relationship, we will look into ways of strengthening the social bonds.[2]

The first is belief in the values and mission of the group. Belief in the overall values allows the individual to get past immediate issues that may present the individual with difficult choices, choices that are made easier by the belief in an overall guiding principle. The second element is attachment, which is the bond developed with the individuals within the group. The more attachments to the group, the more influence the group's approval or expectations will exert on individual behavior. The third element is commitment and represents the depth of the attachments to the group and manifests itself through the resources an individual commits to the success of the group. The types of resources include measurable items like time and effort, but to the extent that an individual's commitment is made public and therefore develops an association between the individual and the group, the committed resources can be leveraged to benefit of the group and individual. Finally, the last element is involvement with various activities within the group. Involvement gives the individual a broader perspective and appreciation of the group's values and mission and, in an ethical organization, promotes positive behaviors.

We further discussed that by group, we are really looking at two distinct settings, both of which provide opportunity and risk. The first setting is the overall business atmosphere in the organization. This encompasses all the high-level perceptions of the work environment, including reputation, mission, vision, and values—what we termed in the last chapter as the cause—and culture. These are the impressions and information that an employee derives indirectly. These impressions are formed by what your employees hear or read from third parties, whether the third party is a person, publication, or the rumor mill.

The second setting is the small group. These are the people who the individual interacts with regularly within the organization. In the majority of cases, people will interact with others who are part of a specific functional area, such as the finance department, but this category will also include those outside the immediate physical environment and extends to contacts throughout the organization. So while most interaction will be physically proximate, certain groups, like human resources or internal audit, have extensive contacts outside their department. The critical distinguishing feature is that information comes to the employee directly through what the employee observes. We further discussed the special case of managers and leadership, but will save that discussion for the next chapter.

BELIEF

Much of the groundwork for our discussion on belief was laid in Chapter 9. Humans are social animals and we have a desire to be accepted and liked by those around us. This applies to lifelong friends and to complete strangers alike. In social control theory, belief is usually addressed as the last element primarily because belief in the context of criminal psychology applies to societal norms. In the context of criminal behavior, societal norms are relatively established and agreed on. For our purposes, the "cause" of the organization may not even be known, let alone agreed on.

We talk of belief in a corporate cause in the manner of the cause of the British abolitionists of the nineteenth century—a rally point for strangers. In criminology, as members of society we all have a vested and common interest in minimizing criminal behavior. Employees in an organization do not necessarily have a vested or common interest in success beyond their own continued employment. Which may be enough—millions of employees arrive to work, do a fine job, and leave without needing to rally under the corporate banner. And they do so in an ethical manner day in and day out. What building a "belief" in the cause of the organization does is strengthen the ethical fabric of your organization for those times when ethics will be tested.

The vision, mission, and values of the organization also serve two other purposes if done correctly. The first is that a well-known organization cause will attract employees who are interested in the vision, mission, and values of the organization. The more the cause of the organization becomes known and associated with the organization, the more the organization is able to attract employees who will espouse and conform to the organizational cause. Further, the right cause can develop an organization reputation in the mind of the public and create a well of goodwill that can serve the company in times of trouble.

I FLY SWA

The mission of Southwest Airlines (SWA) is "dedication to the highest quality of Customer Service delivered with a sense of warmth, friendliness, individual pride, and Company Spirit."[3] While customer service and dedication to the customer experience forms the basis of many a mission statement, for Southwest it is the mission statement. Further, the way it delivers the highest-quality customer service is articulated in clear terms: warmth, friendliness, and pride. These attributes have also become part of the Southwest brand in the minds of the consuming public: Southwest Airlines has consistently ranked highest in customer satisfaction and lowest in terms of complaints per passengers boarded of major domestic carriers since September 1987, the year the Department of Transportation began tracking customer satisfaction statistics. Further, it is consistently ranked as one of the most admired companies in *Fortune* magazine's annual poll.[4]

Like Jordan's Furniture discussed in the previous chapter, Southwest's corporate personality was built in large part on the personality of its cofounder and longtime chief executive officer, Herb Kelleher. A lawyer by trade, Kelleher may be P. T. Barnum at heart. In 1992, Southwest launched an ad campaign around the slogan "Just Plane Smart." As it turns out, the slogan "Plane Smart" had been in use for over a year by a small aviation company in South Carolina called Stevens Aviation. Where other companies might have lawyered up, Stevens Aviation proposed to settle the dispute the old fashioned way: a one-on-one arm wrestling match between company representatives. Kelleher accepted and the match took place in Dallas in a sports arena.

The companies agreed that it would be a three-round match and the loser in each match would donate $5,000 to charity. For round one, Kelleher introduced a stand-in: a former Texas state arm wrestling champ. Stevens CEO Kurt Herwald was soundly defeated. For round two, Herwald introduced his stand-in: a petite customer service representative who defeated Kelleher easily. When round three was complete, Herwald beat Kelleher, but agreed to allow Southwest Airlines to use the slogan in their advertising. What could have devolved into a legal wrestling match ended up providing $15,000 to charity, a great story, and a tremendous amount of goodwill for the two companies.

Southwest has not always had smooth air. In early 2008, the Federal Aviation Administration (FAA) fined Southwest over $10 million for safety violations, which were initially reported by the airline itself. After initially calling the fines "unfair," Southwest Chairman Gary Kelly struck a more conciliatory tone when internal reviews revealed that Southwest flew uninspected planes and that levels of safety were not up to Southwest's standards. Further, questions were raised regarding the relationship between Southwest employees and FAA officials and whether prior professional association caused the FAA to extend preferential treatment to Southwest. Three Southwest employees were placed on administrative leave and investigations continue. Despite the turbulence, the public has seemed very forgiving: Southwest ranked at the top of domestic passengers carried year-to-date in September 2008, experiencing a slight increase year-to-year relative to a slight decline for the domestic industry as a whole.

Southwest Airlines has a corporate cause that its employees believe in and demonstrate to customers. It has developed a tradition of values surrounding its approach to its business that are clearly articulated throughout the company and publicly through advertising and other outreach efforts. By doing so, it has developed an engaged workforce with a public reputation for being fun and it has earned the goodwill of the consuming public.

ATTACHMENT

Once the beliefs of the organization are established, the next step in engaging the employee is to develop the attachment between the employee and the organization. Attachment should be fostered on both the macrolevel—with the organization—and at the microlevel—with the employee's immediate functional area. Attachment is emotional and so we are looking for the employee to connect with the group, to internalize its beliefs and values, and to develop a mutual respect between the employee and the groups. Connection is a result of feeling that the employee is a part of the organization and the functional group. It means that an employee has both job satisfaction and job contribution—that they are getting something from their work and giving something meaningful in return. Internalizing the corporate cause implies the employee subscribes to the way the organization conducts itself and conducts him or herself in a similar manner. Finally, mutual respect means that the employee's view of the organization is important and how the organization views the employee is important.

Establishing emotional attachment starts with the corporate cause and the positive perception resulting from a vision, mission, and values that the employee can admire. The cause establishes a reason for the employee to be attracted to the organization and maintain the attraction throughout their employment. The cause also establishes a standard to evaluate the employee's actions and the actions of others in the organization, management in particular. A critical part of the attachment process is to firmly believe that the organization is fair. The simplest measure of "fairness" in an organization is to observe, to the extent possible, the actions of the management to determine if there is a double standard.

If its leadership lives the values espoused by the organization, the employee will begin to build trust in them and the organization. Trust, as we have discussed, is the critical building block of an organization and a necessity for employee engagement. Trust of leadership is also very difficult to establish, especially in large organizations where the chances of personal contact between leadership and employees can be small. According to BlessingWhite, just over one-half of all employees trust senior management.[5] For the organization, establishing trust is first and foremost about perception and, for an organization committed to its values, making certain that its commitment to its values are accurately communicated throughout the organization. Mistrust festers in environments where information is scarce. Leadership needs to reach out to employees and find out what information they need to feel comfortable that leadership is committed to and lives the values of the organization. With a base level of trust in the organization and the management, the employee will form the attachments necessary for engagement.

COMMITMENT

The next stage for an employee after attachment is ever greater commitment to the organization. In the attachment stage, the organization made efforts to communicate to the employee that the organization stands for something worthwhile, that the organization is committed to its cause, and that leadership at all levels adhere to those values and standards. The commitment stage is the employee's reciprocal effort on behalf of the organization. The goal of the organization is to deepen the connection with the individual employee so that they cease to be just an employee and become a representative of the organization. By being a representative, the employee has completed the internalization of the corporate values and is ready to give back.

The commitment stage represents an investment of resources to make a positive contribution to the organization. For the most part, the resources invested will be measured by time and effort resulting in a large increase in productivity. But in addition, it is important to begin to publicly tie the employee with their functional area and the organization as a whole. So the employee becomes associated with General Electric *and* GE Oil & Gas *and* the Lean Quality Group in Florence, Italy. Publicity enhances the employee's investment of time and effort. The more an individual's time and effort is publicly tied to a group, the less likely the individual will engage in behavior detrimental to the group. Publicity turns the resources of time and effort into association, which further deepens the commitment to the group at every level.

The organization, for its part, needs to create a structure to nurture and support the individual employee's increased investment of resources. The organization needs to make sure there are additional and productive outlets for the effort. Supporting resources allocated to the employee's time and effort show appreciation to the employee and send a message to other employees that the organization values the commitment. Furthermore, the organization must communicate with the employee to acknowledge the employee's commitment and express appreciation for that commitment. At a minimum, the employee's manager should communicate the appreciation, but the organization should promote communication from higher leadership that the leadership is aware and values the employee's effort. Finally, the organization should create avenues for public expression of the employee's commitment.

Now is the time to note that what is being described is an iterative process between the organization and its employees. It is also a process that does not occur overnight: Like any relationship, the relationship between the organization and its employee takes time to grow. In the first step, the organization sets the standard for the partnership through the establishment of its corporate cause through the articulation of its vision, mission, and values. This step lays the foundation for everything to come. The next step is that the organization integrates the cause into the workings of the organization and communicates the standard to the employee to evaluate. Effective communication and demonstration of leaderships' commitment to that standard in the organization and in themselves as leaders establishes a trust with the employee. Trust is the foundation of the employee's attachment to the organization and gives the employee comfort that an investment of effort and time in the organization will not go to waste. The next step is the employee's investment of resources to the betterment of the organization. This signals that the employee is ready to make a more substantial commitment to the organization and move beyond being just an employee to being a representative of the company. The organization's role in this step is to support and reward that commitment. If the employee is ready to make a commitment, but there are no avenues to do so or if the effort goes unacknowledged, the employee will no longer engage with the organization and may regress. If the structures are in place, however, the employee and the organization are ready for the next step.

INVOLVEMENT

With a commitment between the employee and the organization, both are ready to work together for the betterment of the organization. Involvement is the partnership that evolves from the iterative process of belief, attachment, and commitment. Here, the employee now moves from being a representative to being an evangelist for the organization, both internally and externally. The employee is now ready to take a greater leadership role in the company and the company wants the employee to take a greater leadership role. Leadership is not simply leadership in title, but in function as well. That said, involved employees are the best source of developing leadership within the organization, and leadership roles that are filled with involved employees will foster higher performance and incent employees to become involved. High-performing organizations have mechanisms, whether formal or informal, to seek out and reward involved employees with leadership roles.

Involved employees will look for roles beyond the job description to enhance the performance of others. Involved employees will be mentors to others. Most important, involved employees will seek ways to make interactions with other stakeholders more efficient by exchanging ideas and information. The organization can promote this by promoting cross-functional activities and, of course, rewarding successful efforts. While the short-term benefit may involve savings or efficiency, the long-term benefit is the establishment of trust across the organization. Cooperation toward a common objective cultivates trust regardless of the size of the monetary savings or efficiency. Finally, involved employees will make strong public commitments on behalf of the organization. In addition to common stakeholders, such as shareholders, customers, and vendors, the organization now has an ally within the community "promoting" the organization through their associations.

IN THE TRENCHES

There are differences between establishing a relationship between the employee and the greater group depending on if we are talking about the organization as a whole or the smaller functional group. The closer and more frequent the interaction between the employee and members of the group, the faster the relationship can evolve—or be destroyed. It goes without saying that line management is a critical part of the relationship between the employee and the organization.

If that relationship is dysfunctional or poor, it is extraordinarily difficult for the organization to overcome. The good news is that the level of trust between employees and their managers is fairly high. According to BlessingWhite, 75 percent of employees trust their immediate supervisor. Since senior leadership constitutes a manager for someone and we are speaking of averages over a large sample, it stands to reason that the difference between the trust level of managers and senior leadership cited earlier in the chapter is proximity and personal contact. One last point is that the counterexample does not hold. An effective manager can overcome poor organizational leadership for a time.

With this in mind, an organization that has a flatter hierarchy, broader functional areas, and is not physically dispersed has an advantage in creating an engaged workforce. An organization that does not have these attributes requires a greater outreach effort to support engagement goals. In particular, it places a greater burden on communications and other efforts to establish connections between parts of the organization. An organization that is more dispersed will also rely much more on the strength of its overall organizational cause and the leadership's commitment to that cause.

WHY ARE WE DOING THIS?

Much of the benefits described have been articulated in terms of organization performance, rather than ethics. As with every task undertaken by an organization, developing a positive relationship between the organization and its employees should not be done for any other reason than to enhance the performance of the organization for the benefit of all stakeholders. Employees that have bonded or engaged with the organization are better performers and longer-term employees. Organizations that have an engaged workforce also perform better. According to research done at the behest of the Values Centre, a portfolio of the "best employers" of January 1998 generates an average annual return of 14 percent through 2005, more than doubling the market return. This portfolio outperforms industry-matched and characteristics-matched benchmarks. It yields a monthly four-factor (adjusting for market returns, size, value, and momentum) alpha of 0.7 percent. When the portfolio contains only companies from the top 50 "best employers," the average annual return is 17.3 percent and the monthly four-factor alpha is 0.9 percent. Investing in employee satisfaction pays off eventually in terms of market valuation.

But the process of establishing a worthwhile cause, creating an environment for attachment to the organization, receiving a commitment from the employee, and getting the employee involved in promoting the organization all serve to create a powerful deterrent to unethical behavior: a *stake in conformity*. The stronger the bond your employees have with your organization and the greater the investment the employee has made in your organization's success, the greater the stake the employee has in ensuring nothing threatens that relationship. A strong partnership between the organization and its employees will not only make it less likely that any given employee will violate their ethical responsibilities, but it also creates an incentive for employees to make sure that the malicious behavior of others does not threaten the relationship and investment.

THE WHOLE PICTURE

In this chapter, we discussed how an organization can use the elements of social control theory to strengthen the partnership between the employee and the organization. Because humans are social animals and the majority of people—including your employees—operate on the social sphere of moral development, they have a natural inclination to seek approval from those they like and respect. By understanding the psychology of the relationship between an individual and the group, we learn what is necessary to promote a strong, healthy relationship between your organization and its employees that will inure them to the benefit of both.

The first is belief in the values and mission of the group. We laid the groundwork for understanding how to rally individuals of diverse background to a cause in Chapter 9, and in this chapter we examined the more practical aspect of belief in the overall values and principles of an organization. The belief serves to establish a standard of desired behavior and becomes the organizational moral compass that becomes internalized by employees. The organizational cause is the beginning of the process of developing a strong partnership with your employees.

The second element is attachment that is the bond developed with the individuals within the group. Attachment should be fostered with the organization with the employee's immediate functional area. Successful attachment results in a connection with the group and the internalization of its beliefs and values. The employee feels a part of the organization and the functional group. Attachment means that an employee has job satisfaction and is willing to contribute to the job. Finally, with attachment, the employee begins to trust the organization. Trust is the most important building block of an organization and without trust the organization can never form a lasting relationship with the employee.

The third element is commitment and represents the depth of the attachments to the group and manifests itself through the resources an individual commits to the success of the group. The types of resources include measurable items like time and effort, but to the extent that an individual's commitment is made public and therefore develops an association between the individual and the group, the committed resources can be leveraged to benefit of the group and individual. It is important to understand that building the bond between the organization and the employee takes time. At this stage, the employee is ready to become more involved with the organization. Involvement gives the individual a broader perspective and appreciation of the group's values and mission and, in an ethical organization, promotes positive behaviors. Involved employees seek leadership roles and should become a source to develop leaders for the organization.

Each organization is unique, so there are no simple formulas for creating a successful bonding process. The elements, though, are common. First and foremost, the organization must establish trust through effective communication between the organization and its employees and demonstrable adherence to the organization's cause. Second, the organization must establish mechanisms for the employee to contribute beyond the immediate job function. Doing so develops the employee professionally and gives the employee an understanding of how their actions contribute to the success of the organization. Finally, public association and recognition strengthens the bonds between the employee and the organization. While a successful bonding between the employee and the organization will have a positive impact on your organization's performance, from our perspective, a partnership with the employee creates a stake in conformity or a powerful disincentive to engage in deviant behavior. The stronger the bond your employees have with your organization and the greater the investment the employee has made in your organization's success, the greater the stake that employee has in ensuring nothing threatens that relationship. The result is an environment that encourages ethical behavior and creates deterrents for unethical behavior.

NOTES

1. This story was overheard at a baseball game. Its veracity cannot be verified, but is not in doubt.
2. Those familiar with employee engagement will also recognize elements from Chapter 6 as being components of a successful engagement program.
3. Southwest Airlines, "The Mission of Southwest Airlines," *Southwest.com.* Available from http://www.southwest.com/about_swa/mission.html (accessed 21 January 2009).
4. "America's Most Admired Companies 2008," *CNNMoney.com.* Available from http://money.cnn.com/magazines/fortune/mostadmired/2008/champions/index.html (accessed 19 January 2009).
5. BlessingWhite, "The State of Employee Engagement 2008: North American Overview" (April–May 2008).

CHAPTER 11

How to Develop Leadership

The final test of a leader is that he leaves behind him in other men the conviction and will to carry on.

—WALTER J. LIPPMAN

FORE!

In Chapter 7, we discussed the Smithsonian Institution and the problem of failed leadership. Appreciating the interpersonal dynamics of groups in organizations as iconic as the Smithsonian is particularly difficult, but no more so than any group of passionate, high-achieving, intelligent individuals. In situations where attention is paid, the payoff can be substantial. In November 2006, Paul Azinger was named the captain of the 2008 Ryder Cup team.[1] The Ryder Cup pits American golfers against European golfers in a match play championship. The biannual tournament had been dominated by the Americans since its inauguration in 1927, but in the 11 tournaments since 1985, the Europeans had won seven matches and tied one. While home to the best golfers in the world for four rounds of stroke play, in match play—where a golfer or team of two golfers wins a point by the low score on a hole—the Americans have struggled over the past 20 years. Even Tiger Woods, arguably the greatest golfer of all time, had a losing record in Ryder Cup play.

As (bad) luck would have it, an injury prevented Tiger Woods from playing in 2008, an event that seemed to seal the Americans' fate against the favored Europeans. Yet while golf is the consummate individual sport, Azinger understood that teams win Ryder Cups, not golfers. So Azinger set out to create a great team from this group of great golfers.[2] Azinger insisted on fundamental changes in choosing the team. While the top 10 golfers normally get an automatic invitation with the remaining two chosen by the captain, Azinger pushed for a format with eight automatic bids and four "Captain's Picks." When he understood which eight players he had, Azinger divided the eight into three subteams of four based on similar styles of play, and used his captain's picks to round out the squads. The result was three groups that blended well together, supported each other, and a team victory for the Americans.[3] Paul Azinger changed the culture of the group in order to achieve his goals. His self-confidence, ability to communicate and connect with the players, and his appreciation for the greater challenge of the team enabled him to create the dynamics that allowed the best to come from each player. To their individual credit, each player understood the changes and the challenges before them and responded to Azinger's leadership.

The size of the Ryder Cup "organization" simplified Azinger's leadership task. For sprawling organizations, the leadership task is more complicated. To be successful, executive leadership needs to think broadly when thinking in terms of corporate leadership. Until this point, we have been discussing leadership in the context of executive leadership, but "leadership" is not about titles. Executive leaders need to seek out and support leaders at all levels of the organization. Of course, there are organizations with strong reputations for developing leaders.

CASE STUDY

WHIRLPOOL AND
LEADERSHIP
DEVELOPMENT[4]

Whirlpool Corporation, based in Benton Harbor, Michigan, is a Fortune 500 company and a global manufacturer and marketer of major home appliances, with annual sales of approximately $20 billion, more than 73,000 employees, and more than 70 manufacturing and technology research centers around the world. The company markets household U.S. brand names, including Whirlpool, Maytag, KitchenAid, Jenn-Air, and Amana, as well as international brands, including Inglis, Brastemp, Consul, and Bauknecht, to consumers in nearly every country around the world.

Whirlpool has distinguished itself in the consumer durable goods industry through its commitment to socially responsible business principles and its dedication to developing and sustaining strong corporate leadership. These efforts have resulted in the company being listed in *Business Week*'s "Top 100 Most Innovative Companies," *Business Ethics*'s "100 Best Corporate Citizens," and *Ethisphere*'s "World's Most Ethical Companies." Additionally, the company has been included in a number of socially screened indexes, including the Dow Jones Sustainability North American index, KLD's Global Sustainability index, and the Financial Times Stock Exchange 4Good. All recognized the company for its global corporate responsibility standards. In the area of leadership, Whirlpool has regularly placed in the "Top 20 U.S. Companies for Leaders" ranking. Moreover, Whirlpool has been selected as one of the "Top 50 Most Respected U.S. Companies" by the Reputation Institute and *Forbes* magazine.

What factors have made Whirlpool a leader in responsible business practices and corporate culture in an industry where there are many laggards in these areas? Whirlpool's widely admired corporate culture can be attributed primarily to the company's history of strong leadership and its

(Continued)

dedication to cultivating and advancing its talent. The company is notable for having had only six chief executives in its 93-year history, all of whom were selected from within the company's ranks. Since 2006, Whirlpool has been led by Chairman and CEO Jeff Fettig, who has been credited with boosting the company's share price more than 50 percent, and commended for his approach to talent and strong commitment to the development of leaders. Additionally, Whirlpool has instituted one of the most comprehensive and advanced leadership development programs in the corporate world.

LEADERSHIP STRATEGY

The success of Whirlpool's global business is largely tied to its ability to understand and fulfill customer needs, develop highly innovative branded solutions, and continuously improve productivity and quality. While most of Whirlpool's peers strive toward the same goals, Whirlpool has set itself apart in its successes in these areas. The factor most likely to have contributed to these successes is Whirlpool's unusually strong leadership tradition and commitment to continually developing its executives and managers.

When Jeff Fettig became chairman and CEO, he inherited Whirlpool's legacy of forward-thinking leadership and investment in the company's talent. Whirlpool's previous CEO, David Whitwam, led the company for 17 years and is best known for his 1999 initiative to weave innovation into the fabric of the organization. In 1999, when the company hit hard economic times, instead of cutting costs, Whitwam led a company initiative to integrate a systems approach to innovation into the corporate culture. The initiative resulted in 36 percent growth. Whirlpool's rival, Maytag, took the "traditional" safe route and cut costs instead. In 2006, Whirlpool became the largest appliance manufacturer in the world by acquiring Maytag, ending Maytag's 112-year history as an independent company. Today, Whirlpool is recognized as a global leader in consumer appliance innovation.

Whitwam also notably refused to retire from his position until (1) the company was performing well, (2) there was a seasoned global-leadership team in place, (3) there was an exceptional successor ready to take over as CEO, and (4) the company was supported by a solid operating platform and strategies that were well directed and successfully executed. Therefore, when Whitwam finally relinquished his position at the helm, Fettig took possession of a sound company with excellent prospects. However, had he not pledged to continue the policies of his predecessor and committed to advancing them, Whirlpool could have easily lost ground in terms of both market share and the strength of its corporate culture. To ensure this did not happen, Fettig amplified the message that Whirlpool's strength lay in its human capital and that the company's future depended on its ability to engage and develop its talent: "The best investments that we make to profitably grow our business are in our people. As the world and the business environment have changed dramatically, Whirlpool has made significant changes in its approach to talent and the development of leaders. This recognition is a tribute to the many people at Whirlpool who have contributed to the transformation of our talent and development practices to help us deliver value to our shareholders."[5]

EMPLOYEE AND LEADERSHIP DEVELOPMENT

To make the development and advancement of company leadership a practice rather than mere aspiration, Whirlpool put in place a three-year Leadership Development program, which gives new employees the opportunity to participate in a variety of challenging assignments and further develop their skills. As part of the program, new employees rotate through several positions in the company, including marketing, information technology, finance and accounting, engineering, human resources, and/or supply chain. Another aspect of the program is the employee's participation in

(Continued)

high-level projects that are expected to have a direct impact on the company's success.

Whirlpool also offers an "onboarding boot camp" for new employees consisting of three days of orientation, functional training, and networking sessions. The boot camp gives participants exposure to senior leaders and an understanding of the company's business strategy. Further, new employees also have opportunities to gain global experience either through a global rotation or by working on a global project team or assignment.

At the senior leadership level, Whirlpool follows a leadership strategy based on a 12-attribute leadership competency model. Whirlpool uses a four-step talent scouting process in which they first assess candidates against the leadership model. Then they assess individual performance and potential, rate candidates, and openly and honestly communicate with them about how they fit into the company.

Additionally, new leaders undergo a year of intensive assessment and monitoring, aggressive feedback, and coaching. They look at the candidate's performance and effectiveness in his or her current job and prepare them for expanded leadership roles. External and internal coaches and mentors give one-on-one coaching. Candidates are also required to write a vision letter that outlines what they think being chief executive of Whirlpool means.

Talent management ensures that there is a succession plan for all levels of executive leadership and middle management, and that the leadership pipeline is filled with a diverse pool of qualified leadership candidates who can execute the company's strategy. The company also invests in leadership skill building. Senior leaders are responsible for developing the employees who report to them.

Whirlpool's policies and programs in the talent management and leadership development areas underpin the company's values creation strategy. Since January 2000, Whirlpool has seen its stock rise over 25 percent compared to a less than 1 percent rise in the Dow Jones Industrial Average and a loss of 12 percent for the Standard & Poor's

500. As the company has seen its stock prices increase, and both employee engagement and customer loyalty rise, it is clear that its investments in these areas have generated both the tangible and intangible returns associated with an organization operating in an ethical manner with an emphasis on developing involved employees and leaders that are in the societal sphere.

Whirlpool, of course, is not the only example of a corporation taking leadership development seriously. General Electric, Procter & Gamble, General Mills, McKinsey, and IBM are all known for leadership development, as well as international companies, such as Nokia and Infosys Technologies in Finland and India, respectively.

INVESTING IN THE FUTURE

As senior leadership, there will be no more powerful or positive decision you will make than to invest in your leadership. Hopefully, what we have discussed so far is intuitive. The two questions that most often come up are "How do we find leaders?" and "Well, Whirlpool has a lot of money, but my business does not have those resources. What do I do?" The first question is actually easier to answer than you would believe: The leaders will find you. The answer to the second question is that an organization can provide many opportunities to develop leadership without the formal programs available to large companies.

The very definition of *leader* indicates that unknown leaders in your organization will come forward if given the opportunity. They want to lead and take charge. They want to succeed and have the organization succeed. They want to have an impact and are looking for the chance to do all of the above. The opportunity is created in several ways. First and foremost, the organization must develop an environment that promotes the bonding model described in Chapter 10: the right cause, attached and committed employees who are ready to become more deeply involved in the organization. In smaller companies, where the financial resources are not available for formal leadership development programs, or there is not a lot of opportunity for cross-functional teams, there are still ways to connect with potential leaders.

To take an example, a software company that had grown rapidly in recent years and was on the verge of further expansion was looking inward to develop and promote new leaders in the organization. The company saw its culture as unique and was particularly sensitive to maintaining the atmosphere it had developed. Yet the increase in the number of employees, changes in responsibility of long-time employees, shift in business emphasis, and other dynamic factors had fundamentally altered the landscape in the employee base, which meant that the company's demographics were changing rapidly. The CEO wanted to ensure that whatever change occurred happened within the framework of his vision and to do that he needed to promote leadership consistent with the corporate ideals.

The CEO considered it best to rely on the judgment of the executive team. First, the CEO told the executive leaders in his organization to get out of their offices and get into the company. They needed to say hello and get to know the work force better, to meet new people and reestablish old friendships. As this happened, the full effect of the growth of the company became more apparent; in particular, in the changing responsibilities of the old guard. Further, the CEO made it a point to send out the executive team in groups of two to the cafeteria during lunch and, occasionally, to the local watering hole after hours. The "groups of two" were critical in that it doubled the chance that the executives would have a connection with the employee group and it allowed one executive to *listen* and *observe* while the other is speaking. Armed with questions as simple as "What do you do?"; "What company did you work for before coming here?"; and "Do you like it here?" the effort provided copious amounts of internal information and reminded the executive team that internal stakeholders were being taken for granted.

The outreach program produced very good results, though not all good news. The executive leadership found the employees shared their concerns about the changing atmosphere and found that the employees believed the leadership had lost touch. The news was understandable given the circumstances, but difficult to hear. Most important at that point in the company's history, the personal touch by the executives conveyed a message to the employee base. The outreach also yielded a few individuals who the current executive team felt were ready for more significant leadership roles. The question was what to do.

Broadly, Paul Azinger, the Ryder Cup captain, was correct in focusing on breaking up a large group into smaller, more manageable units, identifying what he had to work with and what he needed to fill in the holes. In this case, first and most important, the executive team identified what specific leadership needs were required as the company grew. Whether it was a division that became large enough to warrant its own controller or a plant that was being built, the team identified significant needs over the next two years. Second, it matched needs to the strengths and weaknesses of the group to make initial assessments on who would be most successful in those positions. If there was no immediate fit, either for a person or a position, the company can develop a "bench" for those employees at the top of mind. The result was a dramatic increase in employee bonding, though the whole process took almost 18 months.

EMERGING LEADERS

When we discussed the social bonding model in Chapter 10, we looked at the way employees first believed in the corporate cause as a first step, attached to the organization as the next step, became committed to the organization in step three, and, finally, became involved by applying their efforts across a broad spectrum of the organization's activities. When the employee has reached the involvement stage, the organization should have ample opportunities within the organization for the employee to work with other groups or on projects outside of their immediate responsibility. While the types of opportunities may vary in importance and depth, the secondary benefits at this stage should be obvious: These opportunities provide a forum for evaluating future leaders. To reiterate, by "leaders" we do not necessarily mean the CEO or executives, but leaders at whatever level the organization needs. Meaningful cross-functional opportunities provide opportunities for evaluating leadership. The Committee to Lease a New Copier for the Fourth Floor will not.

A brief aside might be appropriate at this point. With the limitations of print and the amount of material covered, certain generalizations are necessary to make the broad point that will be important 90 percent of the time. In this case, it is essential to keep in mind that, as was mentioned in Chapter 2, not all individual stakeholders are equal or equally important. A day trader is not as an important investor to a company as a long-term shareholder. Likewise, there are customers with whom you conduct transactions and those with whom you have relationships. In the employee base, it is clear there are traders and investors and that distinction is important for leaders to recognize. Wasting resources on traders in any stakeholder group is nonproductive at best and counterproductive at worst. Likewise, providing an opportunity for involved employees to broaden their knowledge and "try out" their leadership skills may lead to a situation where an employee does not measure up. At that point, you move on.[6] Fair and honest feedback is important for that employee, the other employees watching how the organization conducts itself, and as a "best practice" for the organization, but you move on.

Whirlpool's success in creating the next generation of leaders lay in providing meaningful opportunities for involved employees to broaden their knowledge of the company and their operational skills. In both the case of Whirlpool and the software company, the organizations were as proactive as resources allowed. Whirlpool had the resources to put processes and programs in place to formalize leadership development. The software company relied on the time and personal effort of the executive team to gain a deeper understanding of the company. In each case, the organization uses what resources it has and it works. Just like the software company would find it difficult to commit resources in the manner Whirlpool does, Whirlpool would find it difficult to send top executives into the field to break bread with all 73,000 employees. The objective and result were similar, but the means to achieve them were very different.

A BIAS

There is a pretty clear bias here for promoting from within. Make that an unapologetic bias. There will certainly be circumstances where an organization must go outside to find leadership to place in new roles or as a replacement for an existing spot. But going to the marketplace for leadership talent, especially executive talent, is a riskier proposition. Needless to say, an evaluation of external candidates should be based on the same criteria you look for in internal candidates with simply more faith placed in third-party input and gut feel. Consistently going outside of the organization for new leadership is a sign of a problem.

Developing authentic leaders is a sign of a healthy organization. For most organizations, leadership development is the final result of an overall approach that looks at the way the individuals within the organization and the organization itself—overall and at each level—interact. The approach requires a certain foundation provided by the structure put in place to create a group environment that promotes ethical behavior and establishes strong ties with the organization. By approaching leadership development in this way, you can be assured that the leaders emerging from this process will provide a level of ethical leadership necessary to ensure to the extent possible your organization will minimize the chance of deviant behavior and provide the environment for success in the market.

■ NOTES

1. The Captain of the Ryder Cup is typically a nonplayer.
2. As portrayed in the 2004 Disney film, *Miracle*, which chronicles the 1980 U.S. Olympic hockey team, Coach Herb Brooks ignores the performance of the players at tryouts and submits a list to Walter Bush, the Executive

Director of USA Hockey. When Bush protests that Brooks has not seen the kids play, Brooks replies, "I'm not looking for the best players, I'm looking for the right ones."

3. John Paul Newport, "Team USA's Management Victory," *Wall Street Journal*, September 27–28, 2008, p. W9.

4. A special thanks to Wendy Williams, who researched and drafted this case study.

5. Alejandro Bodipo-Memba, "Leader's Focus on Workers Lifts Share Price, Earns Honor," *Detroit Free Press*, October 21, 2007.

6. In certain cases, external training on leadership development may help.

CHAPTER 12

The Logic of William of Ockham

The aspects of things that are most important to us are hidden because of their simplicity and familiarity.

—LUDWIG WITTGENSTEIN

LAW OF PARSIMONY

While he is known for a theory on simplicity, William of Ockham was a deep and complex thinker. A fourteenth-century Franciscan friar, William was one of the most preeminent philosophers of the Middle Ages. He is, of course, famous for his logical principle "*Entia non sunt multiplicanda praeter necessitatem.*" While the loose translation ends up being something to the effect of "all other things being equal, the simplest solution is the best," what William was saying was slightly different. A solution does not have to be simple, but one should not add any elements to the solution that are not absolutely necessary. The basic elements of creating an ethical organization are simple, though not easy: Focus on the individual at the point of decision, create an environment that compels ethical behavior throughout the organization, and employ leaders who exemplify the behaviors you want practiced. Deviate from these elements and the chances of mis-behavior increase.

In the previous chapters, we have tried to take this approach. With case studies and anecdotes, we looked at the root causes—the human causes—of unethical behavior. To say "You must be ethical in all your dealings" or "It is not what you do but how you do it" is all well and good, but the vast majority of us have been "raised right." We have been taught right from wrong. Humankind goes through life day after day not cheating, not stealing, and generally not misbehaving. The challenge as leaders in organizations is that circumstances will arise—rare, but not rare enough—where a combination of individual susceptibility and lack of structured deterrence combine to give rise to bad behavior. It is at precisely that moment where you want to make sure every influence on that person is positive. At that moment, you can be certain that the individual will not be influenced by some empty slogan or mass-produced poster saying, "Integrity is all you have." At that moment, you want him to understand fully that the right decision is the only acceptable decision to him and the organization.

Is It the Means or the Ends?

While there are many good reasons relating to the betterment of individuals and mankind in promoting business ethics, at its core, business ethics is about high-performance companies. Business ethics is about the structural health of an organization and the ability of an organization to outperform its competition. Integrating ethics into the fabric of your organizations gives you an advantage over the competition in the marketplace of products, ideas, and people. Your organization can reduce the cost of doing business, not just in terms of reduced risk of lawsuits, fines, or other costs of malfeasance, but by reducing natural impediments that arise from a dysfunctional environment.

Further, ethical organizations are attractive to the marketplace and, arguably, attract business at a premium. The *trust premium* is that portion of the price a consumer is willing to pay to avoid a risk of a substandard product or service. We should note the difference between the trust premium and a premium paid for products such as organic produce or green products. The former is founded in the basic business desire to engage in a transaction with a party who will keep up their end of the deal. The latter is based on an individual's personal view (traditional farming is bad) or altruism (helping the planet). So while you may have the best intentions of creating an ethical atmosphere at your organization, business ethics is about enhancing organizational performance.

THE WHOLE VIEW

While we have tried to avoid too much "let's all join hands and sing 'Kumbaya' while we improve the world" in our discussion, it is important for each organization to take an enterprise approach to building value in its business. Value creation in a capitalist society is dependent on a variety of different players, each of whom adds to the organization and plays a role. An organization must take care to identify true stakeholders in the organization, be they owners, shareholders, donors, students, employees, vendors, customers, communities, or any number of specific entities. A *true stakeholder* is a stakeholder who will participate in the success of the organization and can be called on to help the organization in difficult times. Identifying stakeholders is an important first step in focusing the organization to develop is vision, mission, and values, but identifying stakeholders can be challenging particularly in not-for-profit environments.

Beyond the notion of true stakeholders having a permanent interest in the organization, we should recognize there are different levels of commitment and expectations on the part of stakeholders. Not every stakeholder has an equally deep commitment to the organization, nor will the burden of difficult times fall equally on all stakeholder groups. Furthermore, certain stakeholders are transitional stakeholders or entities that may be true stakeholders for a short period of time depending on circumstances at that moment. In each and every case, cultivating and enhancing stakeholder relations is crucial to the success of an organization and an important part of building an ethical environment or navigating an ethical challenge.

So building an ethical organization reaps a greater reward than simply the prevention of malfeasance. Recent research indicates a direct correlation between the performance of companies built on a strong ethical foundation and superior performance in the market-place. The benefits are not just a greater return on investment, but manifest in brand recognition, sales, customer satisfaction, customer loyalty, employee productivity, employee satisfaction, and even re-duced regulatory burdens.

ALL ORGANIZATIONS ARE BUSINESSES

With the flow of information increasing each moment, events can have an immediate and long-lasting impact on an organization's repu-tation and how it is perceived in the marketplace, community, and among its stakeholders. Many organizations not classically considered for-profit businesses significantly rely on reputation and standing in their industry. Universities, professional firms, and nonprofits enjoy the economic and social benefits of a positive reputation as much as corporations. Lapses in ethics in for-profit corporations grab the headlines, but ethical lapses are hardly the exclusive purview of busi-nesses. Academia, nonprofits, and, of course, government all face issues with ethics lapses.

While individual and group behavior is similar across organiza-tions, there are many differences in the circumstances at noncorpo-rate organizations that make resolution difficult. In a corporate entity, there is often more direct power over people and operations that has the benefit of focusing responsibility and accountability at the top. In noncorporate entities, power can be distributed or limited in such a way to make direct control of leadership difficult. There may also be certain groups that wield influence disproportionate to their actual authority or responsibility. While found in for-profit companies, these situations are a more common problem in the not–for–profit sector. Regardless of the situation, ethical lapses hurt *all* types and sizes of organization, not just those looking to make a profit. In the end, those organizations depending on reputation, or those trying to develop a reputation, are especially vulnerable to the consequences of ethical lapses.

CASE STUDY   **UNIVERSITY VERSUS NATION**

Sometimes, there is no good answer to the ethical issue in front of us. While Hiram Bingham III was born in Hawaii, his pedigree was as New England as they come. A descendant of colonists who settled in Connecticut in 1650, Bingham returned from Hawaii to attend Phillips Academy and Yale University where he received his Bachelors in 1898. He later received his Ph.D. from Harvard and later taught at Harvard and Princeton. Hardly the staid Yankee, Bingham had flair and imagination. He lived in the largest house in New Haven and had married an heiress to the Tiffany fortune. While he initially taught college, he quickly became bored.

In late 1906, Bingham sailed to South America to follow the route Simón Bolivar, whom Bingham studied, had taken in 1819. This and subsequent travels were published in various accounts and ignited in Bingham a desire to go back farther in South American history and explore the Incan culture. From 1908 to 1909, Bingham traced the old Spanish trade routes and was reputed to have run into two members of Butch Cassidy's Hole-in-the-Wall Gang. In 1911, Bingham again set out for South America, this time as the Director of the Yale Peruvian Expedition. This trip proved very fruitful to the amateur archeologist. Bingham located the site of the last Inca capital and was the first to ascend the 21,763-foot Mt. Coropuna, the third highest mountain in Peru. Later on that year, Bingham made his most consequential discovery the "lost city" of Machu Picchu.

(Continued)

Located 8,000 feet above sea level, Machu Picchu was built around the year 1460 when the Incan Empire was at the height of its power. Because of its remote location, Machu Picchu escaped the plundering of the Spanish conquistadors. While its exact use is still unknown—a citadel, religious center, trade center, and the estate of the emperor Pachacuti have all been posited—it has become one of the most important archeological sites for the Incan culture and one of the most famous in the world.

The next year, Bingham was back on behalf of *National Geographic* and Yale University to excavate Machu Picchu. The result was some 1,600 artifacts that were tagged and ready to be shipped back to Yale. But the Peruvian government was increasingly unhappy with the arrangement, as more and more Peruvians began to understand what was happening. After some negotiation, the artifacts left Peru and headed for New Haven. What was negotiated came to a head when Yale's Peabody Museum put on an exhibition of artifacts from Machu Picchu. Peruvians were upset that they had to travel to view objects of their heritage and wanted the artifacts back. The Peruvian government contends that the artifacts were lent to Yale. Yale's position was equally clear. Yale contends that all items lent to Yale were returned in the 1920s and the items on display were property of Yale University.

The issue is not unique. Before the advent of modern archeology, antiquities were routinely plundered by looters and amateur archeologists. The buying and selling of antiquities continues. In May 2008, Spanish police recovered 700 pieces of pre-Columbian art stolen from archeological sites in Colombia, Ecuador, and Peru. The monetary allure is great: On July 20, 1985, treasure hunter Mel Fisher found the *Nuestra Señora de Atocha* in 55 feet of water off the Florida Keys. The Spanish galleon contain over 40 tons of silver and gold, including over 100,000 Spanish silver coins ("pieces of eight"), gold coins, emeralds, silver, and gold artifacts and over 1,000 silver bars with an estimated value of $450 million. There are more to be found. Somewhere off the Colombian port of Cartagena lies the *San José*, another Spanish galleon. Sunk by the English in 1708, the *San José* is reputed to contain treasure worth, by some optimistic estimates, $10 billion. An American explorer claims to know where it is, the Colombian government claims the treasure is theirs, and the Spanish government would like a seat at the table. Each party seems to have legitimacy in its assertions. The explorer spends time and money to find something that neither Colombia nor Spain had deemed significant enough to make the exploration effort themselves. Colombia's claim, that the wreck lies in their territorial waters, is right. That the treasure is Spain's is also correct.

While the dispute may seem like a purely legal one, the question for our discussion is what is the ethical decision? Should Yale return the artifacts? If Yale's title in the artifacts is legitimate, do they deserve compensation? If so, how much is "priceless" really worth? What is the ethical obligation of Peru to Yale? After all, Bingham was no late-night grave robber and the Peruvian government was aware of the 1912 expedition. The passage of time and the murkiness of international law add to the confusion. With competing, legitimate claims, who is in the right? In situations like the ones described, ethical dilemmas arising *between* organizations are made more complicated in the absence of trust between the parties. Not everyone can arm wrestle for the rights like Herb Kelleher and Kurt Herwald.

The emphasis of ethics in business transactions is nothing new and we do not have to act like Caesar's wife to appreciate, value, and live an ethical life.[1] The idea of upstanding citizenship, morality, ethics, and fairness is so ingrained in us from an early age that it is easy to forget how recently this was not the norm, and in how many places it still is not. Ethics has evolved based on mutual need, because as individual, solitary creatures, humans can only go so far. We are not particularly fast or strong, but we are quite clever. Early in human history it became clear that there was a tremendous benefit in being in a group. Mutual protection was first and foremost, but as labor became more specialized and each member could contribute to the mutual benefit of the group, the first "organizations" formed. So while at some point in our evolutionary past, humans may have tried to be solitary creatures, it was the cooperation between humans that led to the development of life and society as we know them.

With the formation of groups, however, norms of behavior needed to develop as well. As the first woolly mammoth or wild boar came in from the hunt, the question of how to divide the spoils was presented. Whether or not there is some *instinctual* notion of fair play in humans, if the spoils were not divided in a way that benefitted the whole group in the long run, the group would suffer. Looking back at codes and laws from early civilizations, it is clear that deviating from established laws meant a swift and very harsh punishment. Beyond the idea of right and wrong according to the law, early codes included provisions for ethical treatment of family members, servants, and strangers. Ethical behavior has been a societal expectation for over 4,000 years and is the heart of any successful venture.

Within smaller groups, ethical behavior is very important for smooth relations. Thus, family, friends, spouses, and the bowling team develop boundaries of what is acceptable and unacceptable behavior. While this behavior varies between individuals in the relationship and even varies between relationships one individual may have with another, the establishment of an expectation of certain behavior is the first step in long-lasting relationships.

The study of human behavior also has evolved over the years from the general question of what is the "true" nature of man and what is his relationship with society to a more focused psychological study of morality and behavior. Much like cognition develops over the time from when we are born to early adulthood, morality also develops in the same manner. Our moral maturity sets the stage for our decisions over our lifetime. Yet while our moral development may be set, there are immediate influences on behavior that cause "good people to make bad decisions." The application of psychological study of human behavior has given us insight into why good people make bad choices and, more importantly, how to minimize the chance of this occurring.

ALL ABOUT ME

We have tried to develop a framework for the individual decision making at the heart of unethical behavior. At the heart of this framework are the three elements intertwined to create a profile of how susceptible an individual is to misconduct. The first part is the moral maturity of an individual, which forms the general context of the decision-making process. Individuals operate in three spheres of moral maturity, which are based on Kohlberg's Levels of Moral Development. What sphere one resides in is dependent on the primary way one approaches ethical decision making. The lowest level is the self sphere, which focuses only on the individual's own judgment as to what constitutes moral or ethical behavior irrespective of what others think. The most common level is the social sphere, where one bases one's action not only on the individual's own frame of reference, but what constitutes proper behavior among family, friends, and society. Finally, the highest level is the societal sphere, where the individual views actions in a more abstract way and looks at not only what is expected, but what is right for society as a whole. This last group is the least likely to commit fraud and exhibits qualities that are very beneficial to the organization.

Each individual possesses an innate and fairly constant moral framework to evaluate decisions. This framework is tested by the second element of needs deficiencies based on Maslow's Hierarchy of Needs. In particular, safety needs, such as financial security, which are lacking or perceived to be in an individual's life, will cause stress and pressure on the person's moral framework and may lead to misconduct under certain circumstances. The most common manifestation of a perceived needs deficiency is the anxiety related to the threat of sudden unemployment. If the threat of sudden unemployment is due to a circumstance that the employee believes to be beyond their control, such as when the employee does not have the authority to address a situation, but the responsibility for the consequences from failure, trust, and bonds with the organization will be damaged or destroyed and the employee is vulnerable to unethical behavior. The key point: No one is immune from these pressures and every individual is susceptible given an extreme needs deficiency.

CASE STUDY   CHARLES PONZI AND
                                   HIS SCHEME

When one examines the life of Charles Ponzi, it is very difficult to see anything other than a disaster waiting to happen. He was born in Parma, Italy, in 1882 and moved to the United States in 1903. Ponzi was a drifter with ambitions in contrast to his humble origins. While he was gifted with cunning and charm, he was very short on patience. He participated in all sorts of scams in New England and Quebec. He finally found his way to Boston, where, after stints as a dishwasher and waiter—he was fired for short-changing customers—he quite accidently stumbled upon an interesting arbitrage opportunity.

An international reply coupon was a fixed-cost postage stamp that allowed citizens of member nations of the Universal Postal Union to send a reply coupon with a piece of mail for return postage. The critical piece of the puzzle was that while currencies fluctuated, the reply coupon's exchange rate was fixed. If the exchange rate was depressed for a country, say Italy, Ponzi found out he could buy devalued Italian lira, turn them into International Reply coupons, and then convert the coupons into U.S. dollars for a profit of up to 250 percent. It was all perfectly legitimate. Ponzi had found his Holy Grail.

He began talking up his idea to friends and associates with his plan, which seemed like a no-risk situation. Ponzi guaranteed his investors a 50 percent return in 45 days and money started rolling in. Interest was so great that he formed a business enterprise called Securities Exchange Company to formally handle transactions. At first, people invested and in 45 days they were paid off. As word spread, more and more people joined. Those that wanted to cash out were paid, but most rolled over the money as it became due for another. Ponzi hired agents to spread the word and bring in more cash and paid the agents a commission. These agents were the predecessors of the feeder funds that supplied Bernie Madoff with his clients. In July 1920, a run started on the Ponzi empire as people started to question whether Ponzi could actually deliver the returns he promised. Acting as if nothing was wrong, Ponzi paid off everyone who asked and thus depleted his ready cash by $2,000,000. But when people saw that Ponzi paid off, the run stopped and even more people "invested" with Ponzi's company. The situation could not last and on August 12, 1920, Ponzi was arrested with estimated liabilities of $7,000,000 or approximately $72,000,000 today.[2]

The idea behind the most famous Ponzi scheme—he was not the first to use this methodology—was perfectly legitimate. The challenge, which Ponzi knew but his investors did not, was that once you factored in the cost of buying stamps individually and processing them to make the paper profit, the scheme was unworkable. To Ponzi, it did not matter. Ponzi was the prototypical self sphere individual. He had taken in an estimated $10,000,000, but purchased only a negligible amount of reply coupons. While, to the objective observer, any Ponzi scheme must eventually collapse under the weight of its promises, as the cash coming in continued to increase, Ponzi was able to ride the wave for quite some time. Truth be told, if it were not for certain editors of the *Boston Post,* Ponzi's scheme could have lasted significantly longer.

The final element relates to an individual's capacity for introspection. When Ponzi was arrested many of his clients protested, such was his ability to convince people of his story. Like Bernie Madoff some 80 years later, one wonders how Ponzi could continue to go to friends, associates, and strangers alike with the same lie over and over.

Ponzi and Madoff were missing the psychological brakes of self-awareness and self-control that link the psychological framework of the three spheres and the pressures of the needs deficiency. Self-awareness is the individual recognition of their own moral framework and what constitutes right and wrong. In other words, it is whether an individual can look themselves in the mirror honestly. Self-control is the behavior manifestation of this self-awareness and, in most circumstances, acts as an inhibition to bad behavior. The less self-aware an individual is and the less self-control that individual demonstrates increase the possibility that they will make a bad choice.

With this understanding, organizations should develop an environment that exploits this motivation by using its vision, mission, and values to develop an organizational cause to attract the right type of employee and encourage them to perform in an exemplary manner. A cause forms a rallying point for individuals with little else in common. Further, an organizational cause that is reinforced by the culture, environment, and actions of leadership will develop an employee base that is fully engaged with the organization. Employees that are fully engaged will speak well of the organization and promote the organization to others, plan to stay at the organization, and will look for ways to make the organization better, more efficient, and more profitable.

The cause of the organization should authentically represent the organization and its goals. That the vision, mission, and values conforms to some "standard" or is the result of a detailed SWOT analysis is far less important than to find and describe the core canons that drive the business. Start small if necessary, but once defined, make certain policies and procedures explicitly match the principles where possible and in no way proscribe actions or incent behavior inconsistent with the organizational principles. Organizations should undertake fresh, periodic review of the policies and procedures based on the question, "Does this policy or procedure reinforce our vision, mission, and values and contribute to the cause?"

As powerful as a corporate cause can be, it will be undone if employees experience stress and pressure to compromise those principles. The most common and most dangerous ethical risk organizations face is the moral hazard represented by the dissociation of authority and responsibility, which leads to circumstances where the employee feels trapped. In these cases, the employees must assume the consequences of action, but are not empowered with the proper authority to pursue a course of action consistent with the organization's principles: a situation that can easily deteriorate into one where ethics are compromised. Addressing this dilemma requires that an organization and its employees clearly understand the lines of authority and that the organization creates a mechanism for addressing situations where there is a mismatch.

ENJOYING THE KOOL-AID

It is admittedly difficult for organizations, particularly large ones, to be aware of all of the individual circumstances of its employees, but understanding the root cause of deviant behavior is as important as what causes disease. As with disease prevention, taking care of your overall health is as important as understanding the specific pathology of the disease. In the organizational context, taking care of the body's health means understanding the influence of groups on individual behavior and, in particular, what circumstances create environments where unethical behavior is nonexistent. There are two primary groups with which the individual will associate within your organization and, once a bond is formed with the group, the group will be able to exert influence on the individual. The first is the organization itself. The organization establishes its overall core value system and should live this system in their actions. The organization is indirectly represented to the individual through ways not immediately impacting the individual, but influencing the individual's overall understanding and perception of the organization. Direct contact is made by the second influencer, the small group, which is usually composed of an office, a department or other functional group, other employees with whom the individual interacts with as part of their job, and, possibly, social groups. Where the overall organization is an influencing factor, the small group exerts a great deal of peer pressure to conform to the standards established by that group.

The chances that an individual will conform to the behavior of the group are determined by four elements of social control. The first is belief in the values and mission of the group. Belief in the overall values allows the individual to get past immediate issues that may present the individual with difficult choices, choices that are made easier by the belief in an overall guiding principal. The second element is attachment that is the bond developed with the individuals within the group. The more attachments to the group, the more influence the group's approval or expectations will exert on individual behavior.

The third element, commitment, represents the depth of the attachments to the group and manifests itself through the resources an individual commits to the success of the group. The types of resources include measurable items like time and effort, but to the extent that an individual's commitment is made public and therefore develops an association between the individual and the group, the committed resources can be leveraged to the benefit of the group and individual. Finally, the last element is involvement with various activities within the group. Involvement gives the individual a broader perspective and appreciation of the group's values and mission and, in an ethical organization, promotes positive behaviors. A special set of influencers are managers and other authority figures. The combination of power and proximity creates a unique situation of influence on an individual. Psychological experiments indicate a very high degree of conformity to the wishes of an authority figure by individuals even though the individuals understand that their actions may be detrimental. "I was just doing my job" should never be an excuse.

While social control and peer pressure may sound a bit Orwellian, what we mean is that an organization can use the elements of social control theory to strengthen the partnership between the employee and the organization. It is about cooperation, not coercion, and by understanding the psychology of the relationship between an individual and the group, we learn what is necessary to promote a strong, healthy relationship between your organization and its employees. This relationship forms the foundation of an ethical and high-performing company.

Establishing these bonds is different depending on the organization, though the basic parts are common. First and foremost, the organization must establish trust through effective communication between the organization and its employees and demonstrable strict adherence to the organization's cause. Second, the organization must establish mechanisms for the employee to contribute beyond the immediate job function. Doing so develops the employee professionally and gives the employee an understanding of how their actions contribute to the success of the organization. Finally, much like public association by the employee with their employer creates a sense of commitment of the employee to the employer, a public commitment from the employer to the employee further strengthens those bonds. Successful bonding between the employee and the organization creates a "stake in conformity" or a powerful disincentive to engage in deviant behavior. The stronger the bond your employees have with your organization and the greater the investment the employee has made in your organization's success, the greater the stake the employee has in ensuring nothing threatens that relationship. The result is an environment that encourages ethical behavior and creates deterrents for unethical behavior.

CEO AND TRUST

The most successful ethics initiative within an organization can be undone with the wrong leadership. While great ethical leadership does not guarantee an ethical organization, you cannot have an ethical organization with unethical leadership. The right type of ethical leadership can be best described as authentic and should not be confused with those who are great managers but not necessarily authentic leaders. Leadership is about people, while management is about process. Both are important to the organization, but in very different ways. Authentic leadership is built on self-aware-ness, effective communication, connection, and a higher sense of purpose. It should be clear: Not everyone has the intellectual and emotional profile to run your organization. Authentic leaders are those who have the character to succeed in trying times when so many internal and external forces are adversely impacting your organization.

At the very core, authentic leadership is based on a foundation of trust. Self-awareness is trust in one's self. Communication and con-nection builds personal trust between individuals and an appreciation for the organization's impact on the broader community builds trust with outside stakeholders—both present and future. Looking at the role of leadership at the highest abstraction, the most important job of leadership is building and maintaining trust.

Trust is also the foundation of our economic system. While hard to quantify, its impact on our organizations is beyond doubt. Increasing the trust within your organization reduces internal and external costs. Products and services trusted by consumers command price premi-ums in the marketplace. Moreover, the premium your stock price carries over the market value of your net assets is, to a great degree, a measure of the trust the market places on management's ability to perform well in the future.

We discussed how trust reduces risks and uncertainties in transac-tions between individuals and organizations, in whatever forms those transactions take place. Within your organization, oversight costs be-tween 1 and 6 percent of revenues. Oversight is the cost of mistrust, regardless of where that mistrust comes from. While we cannot ever completely eliminate oversight in our organizations, all organizations would benefit from an oversight cost of 1 percent of revenue rather than 6 percent.

External costs related to a lack of trust are more apparent and easier to recognize. Over 70 years ago, Ronald Coase identified several transactions costs associated with using the market. Among these costs are *enforcement costs*, which are the costs associated with making sure the other party lives up to the bargain and enforcing the terms of the contract, if necessary. The less trustworthy the party on the other side of the transaction, the more time and money will be spent on making sure the transaction is fulfilled. A party with a reputation for honest and ethical dealings will see these qualities manifested in lower costs.

The benefits and costs of a consumer trust were vividly on display in our discussion of the Tylenol and Firestone–Ford case studies. In these case studies, we saw the market react to the companies in very different ways. Johnson & Johnson, relying on a strong corporate cause and the ethical leadership of its CEO and executive team, pursued a strategy that relied on rebuilding trust with the consumers and the general public. Most experts wrote off the effort as doomed, but its approach paid off for both the company and, through improved packaging, the consumer. Firestone and Ford selected the rational choice—self-preservation—and lost not only a 100-year-old business relationship, but also lost the confidence—and trust—of the marketplace.

FEEDING THE WOLF

What we have discussed is as straight forward and as simple as losing weight, but like the formula for weight loss, it often requires a change of perspective and approach. It further requires an ongoing commitment, by you and those who follow, to see how you are measuring up. There is a Boy Scout story of an old Cherokee chief who is teaching his grandson about life. "A fight is going on inside me," he said to the boy. "It is a terrible fight and it is between two wolves.

"One is evil—he is anger, envy, sorrow, regret, greed, arrogance, self-pity, guilt, resentment, inferiority, lies, false pride, superiority, self-doubt, and ego.

"The other is good—he is joy, peace, love, hope, serenity, humility, kindness, benevolence, empathy, generosity, truth, compassion, and faith.

"This same fight is going on inside you—and inside every other person, too."

The grandson thought about it for a minute and then asked his grandfather, "Which wolf will win?"

The old chief simply replied, "The one you feed."

Your organization is also the scene of a struggle between influences that will help build and strengthen the organization and those forces that hurt productivity, profits, and your organization's objectives. The winner of this struggle depends on what attributes the organization promotes. No organization ever achieved success by promoting bureaucracy, blame, or retaliation. At the heart of any ethical organization is living the aspects of the organization that will enable long-term success. And doing so will not only make you feel good, it will not only make your organization look good, it will improve your organization's performance across the board.

◾ NOTES

1. To "act as Caesar's wife" has an interesting history. A few years after Julius Caesar married Pompeia in 67 BCE, a scandal occurred during the rites of Bona Dea ("Good Goddess"). The rites were conducted in Caesar's house by Pompeia and Aurelia, Caesar's mother. The ceremony was for women only and no men were allowed. Publius Clodius, a politician of some disrepute, disguised himself as a woman and entered the rites, but was discovered by Aurelia. Rumors linked Pompeia and Clodius in an affair. Caesar divorced Pompeia because "Caesar's wife must be above suspicion."
2. "Ponzi Arrested; Liabilities Out at $7,000,000," *New York Times,* August 12, 1920, p. 1.

Index